Hedge Funds

Hedge Funds

Vikas Agarwal

*Georgia State University,
Robinson College of Business,
35, Broad Street, Suite 1221,
Atlanta GA 30303, USA*

vagarwal@gsu.edu

Narayan Y. Naik

*London Business School,
Sussex Place, Regent's Park,
London NW1 4SA, UK*

nnaik@london.edu

the essence of knowledge

Boston – Delft

Foundations and Trends® in Finance

Published, sold and distributed by:
now Publishers Inc.
PO Box 1024
Hanover, MA 02339
USA
Tel. +1 (781) 871 0245
www.nowpublishers.com
sales@nowpublishers.com

Outside North America:
now Publishers Inc.
PO Box 179
2600 AD Delft
The Netherlands
Tel. +31-6-51115274

A Cataloging-in-Publication record is available from the Library of Congress.

Printed on acid-free paper

ISBN: 1-933019-17-4; ISSNs: Paper version 1567-2395; Electronic version 1567-2409

Contents

Section 1   Introduction   **1**

Section 2   Hedge Fund Performance   **5**

2.1	Risks and rewards: Hedge funds versus mutual funds	5
2.2	Return generating process of hedge funds	7
2.3	Nonlinear payoff structure of hedge funds	9
2.4	Manager skill in hedge funds	14
2.5	Other interpretations of alpha	16
2.6	Persistence in the performance of hedge funds	17
2.7	Market timing ability of hedge funds	21
2.8	Hedge funds and the technology bubble	22

Section 3   Hedge Fund Characteristics and Performance   **23**

3.1	Compensation and performance	23
3.2	Theoretical models on optimal incentive contracts	25
3.3	Managerial flexibility and performance	27
3.4	Fund size and performance	28

3.5   Fund age, manager tenure, and performance | 28
3.6   Hedge fund style and performance | 29

Section 4   Hedge Fund Characteristics and Risk-Taking Behavior   **31**

4.1   Compensation and risk-taking behavior of hedge fund managers | 31
4.2   Hedge fund characteristics and survival | 32

Section 5   Funds of Hedge Funds   **35**

Section 6   Hedge Fund Indices   **37**

Section 7   Determinants of Investors' Money Flows into Hedge Funds   **39**

Section 8   Risk Management in Hedge Funds   **41**

8.1   Risk management and Value-at-Risk (VaR) | 41

Section 9   Systemic Risks from Hedge Fund Activity   **45**

Section 10   Diversification   **49**

10.1   Increasing the number of hedge funds in a portfolio | 50
10.2   Mixing hedge funds with a portfolio of traditional investments | 51
10.3   Optimal hedge fund portfolio | 52

Section 11   Biases   **55**

11.1 Databases   55
11.2 Data accuracy and auditing   56
11.3 Measurement bias   57
11.4 Survivorship bias   58
11.5 Stale price bias   60
11.6 Instant history bias   61
11.7 Self-selection bias   62
11.8 Multi-period sampling bias   62

References   **63**

1

Introduction[1]

In this survey, we attempt to summarize and provide an overview of the academic research on hedge funds and commodity trading advisors (CTAs). The hedge fund industry has grown tremendously over the recent years. It is difficult to accurately estimate the true size of the hedge fund industry since the Securities and Exchange Commission (SEC) imposes restrictions on advertising for hedge funds. One of the hedge fund advisory firms, Hedge Fund Research (HFR), estimates that the total assets under management (AUM) of hedge funds have increased from USD 39 million in 1990 to about USD 972 million in 2004. During this period, the total number of hedge funds has gone up from 610 in 1990 to 7,436 in 2004. Furthermore, the allocation between different hedge fund strategies has also changed significantly during the same period. In 1990, the macro strategy dominated the industry with 71% of total assets under management while in 2004; their share was only 11%. Instead, in 2004, Equity Hedge strategy had the largest share of AUM – 29%.[2] There has also been a shift in the average

[1] N.Y. Naik is thankful to the BNP Paribas Hedge Fund Centre at the London Business School and both authors are very grateful to Maria Strömqvist for excellent research assistance. They are responsible for all errors.
[2] Source: Hedge Fund Research (HFR) – <www.hedgefundresearch.com>

investor in hedge funds from an individual investor to an institutional investor. In the early 1990s, the typical investor was a high net-worth individual investor who invested in macro funds, which then took levered bets on currencies and other assets. Today, the typical investor is an institutional investor, for example a pension fund, which invests in hedge funds for diversification reasons, seeking investment vehicles with low correlation with other traditional asset classes such as equities and bonds.

Though hedge funds have gained popularity in the last fifteen years or so with the rise of star hedge fund managers such as George Soros and Julian Robertson, they have been in existence for more than 50 years now. The first hedge fund is believed to be started by a former Fortune magazine writer named Alfred Winslow Jones. He employed a then novel idea of taking both long and short positions in stocks to "hedge" out the market risk. Using this strategy cleverly by buying undervalued securities and selling overvalued securities, his fund returned a whopping 670% return between May 1955 and May 1965.[3] Although Jones' original fund used "long-short" strategy to hedge, today not all the hedge funds necessarily hedge. In fact, there is no universally accepted definition of hedge funds. They can now be identified by their exemption from the Investment Company Act of 1940 and the unique compensation structure.

Given the enormous growth of this industry and the limited information available on hedge funds, a need for research has emerged from both investors' and regulators' point of view. Investors need research to better understand what they are investing in and what risks they are exposed to. Research on hedge funds may also help investors recognize what diversification benefits, if any, hedge funds offer in combination with investments in equity and bonds. Regulators need research to identify if there is a need for regulation to protect investors' interests and what impact hedge funds may have on the stability of the financial markets.

The rest of the paper is outlined as follows. The first part of the paper summarizes the research on hedge fund performance, including

---

[3] Source: Joseph Nocera, "The Quantitative, Data-Based, Risk-Massaging Road to Riches", *New York Times*, June 5, 2005.

comparison of risk-return characteristics of hedge funds with those of mutual funds, factors driving hedge fund returns, and persistence in hedge fund performance. The second part of the paper covers research regarding the unique contractual features and characteristics of hedge funds and their influence on the risk-return tradeoffs. The third part of the paper reviews the research on the role of hedge funds in a portfolio including the extent of diversification benefits and limitations of standard mean-variance framework for asset allocation. Finally, the last part of the paper summarizes the research on the biases in hedge fund databases.

2

Hedge Fund Performance

There is a large literature on hedge fund performance including comparison of their performance with mutual funds, their return generating process using multifactor models, analysis of their investment styles, nonlinearity of their payoff structure, estimation of manager skill, persistence in their performance, timing ability, and their role in systemic risk and bubbles. We review each of these areas below.

2.1. Risks and rewards: Hedge funds versus mutual funds

Given that hedge funds are loosely regulated and thus being not obligated to disclose information on their investment strategies or returns, it is natural, as a starting point, to try to understand hedge funds by comparing them to something more familiar, like mutual funds. Both hedge funds and mutual funds are investment vehicles but the investment strategies they employ are very different. Mutual funds mainly employ buy-and-hold strategies, where they only take long positions in mostly liquid assets, and their returns are often compared to a benchmark index. Hedge funds employ more dynamic trading strategies, where they usually take both long and short positions in sometimes illiquid assets and they have an absolute return target. These dissimilarities give rise to differences in the risk-return characteristics of these two investment vehicles.

Liang [73] finds that hedge funds have higher returns but also higher risk than mutual funds. The average monthly return during 1992 to 1996 for hedge funds was 1.10% compared to 0.85% for mutual funds. The standard deviation during the same period was 2.40% for hedge funds and 1.91% for mutual funds. Hence, a risk-adjusted performance measure should be used when comparing the two. One such measure is the Sharpe ratio which provides a ratio of the excess return to the total risk. Liang [73] finds that hedge funds have higher Sharpe ratio than mutual funds (on average 0.44 compared to 0.26). This means that the mean-variance frontier is higher for hedge funds than for mutual funds. Ackermann, McEnally, and Ravenscraft [1] also find that the average hedge fund Sharpe ratio is higher than the comparable mutual fund Sharpe ratio (21% higher) and this performance advantage increases when they match funds by region. They also find that the average total risk is 27% higher for hedge funds which mean that hedge funds achieve this Sharpe ratio superiority despite their higher total risk. However, Ackermann, McEnally, and Ravenscraft [1] find mixed results comparing the Sharpe ratios of hedge funds with those of market indices, the former being higher in about 50% of all the cases. This result may be driven by their approach of adjusting the systematic risk through betas. These betas can change frequently due to the use of dynamic trading strategies by hedge funds. In addition, another strand of literature has indicated the shortcomings of Sharpe ratio as a measure of risk-adjusted performance. A number of studies including Fung and Hsieh [43, 48], Amin and Kat [12], and Agarwal and Naik [5] show that hedge fund payoffs are nonlinear due to their use of dynamic option-like trading strategies. Goetzmann, Ingersoll, Spiegel, and Welch [61] show how Sharpe ratio can be manipulated by the use of option-like strategies that can alter the shape of the probability distribution of returns. Further, Lo [78] cautions the use of Sharpe ratios in presence of positive autocorrelation of hedge fund returns that can result in an upward bias in Sharpe ratios.

2.2. Return generating process of hedge funds

In addition to comparing the performance of hedge funds with mutual funds, extant research has also addressed how hedge funds generate returns? The answer to this question should help in benchmarking and classification of hedge funds. Hedge funds take alpha and beta bets to generate their returns. The beta is the return of the fund related to the exposure to different asset classes and the alpha is the return above what is explained by the asset classes. The alpha and beta can be determined using a linear multifactor model, where the return of the hedge fund, is regressed on a number of factors, and where alpha is the intercept of the model.

If all hedge funds were following the original Jones' model of taking both long and short positions, one would expect the betas with respect to the market to be close to zero if they hedge out the market risk completely. This is often termed as "market neutrality" in the hedge fund industry. A fund is said to be market neutral if it generates returns that are uncorrelated with the returns on some market index or a collection of other risk factors such as interest rate, liquidity, and volatility. Non-zero betas mean that hedge funds are different from the original hedge definition, in which combining long and short positions are designed to neutralize market risk. The claim of market neutrality has been tested in several papers.

Liang [73] uses an eight asset-class factor model including factors for equity, debt, currency, commodities, and cash. Using stepwise regression to mitigate potential multicollinearity problem among factors, the result indicates that factor loadings are scattered around different asset classes and different strategies. No single asset class dominates in the regressions with R^2 ranging from 0.20 to 0.77. Hedge funds are found to have low betas with the US equity market, which indicate that hedge funds are less correlated with the market compared to the traditional vehicles such as mutual funds. Patton [89] reaches the same conclusion by using several different definitions of neutrality; mean neutrality, variance neutrality, Value-at-Risk neutrality, and tail neutrality. He concludes that many hedge funds that label themselves as market neutral are in fact not market neutral. However, these funds are more market neutral than other categories of hedge funds.

A special case of linear multifactor models is style analysis proposed by Sharpe [91]. Style analysis also involves a linear asset class factor model with two constraints. The betas (the portfolio weights) must sum to one and they have to be non-negative. Fung and Hsieh [43] apply returns-based style analysis to mutual funds and hedge funds. They find that mutual funds have high correlation with the asset classes while hedge funds have not. While more than half the mutual funds have R-squares above 75%, nearly half of the hedge funds have R-squares below 25% and no single asset class is dominant in the regressions. Unlike mutual funds, a substantial fraction of the hedge funds (25%) is negatively correlated with the standard asset classes. In addition, only 17% of hedge funds have coefficients of the most significant asset class statistically greater than zero and not statistically different from one. Hence, the conventional style analysis cannot be directly applied to hedge funds. Fung and Hsieh [43] propose an extension to Sharpe [91] model for analyzing investment management styles. They state that managers' returns can be characterized by three general determinants: the returns from assets in the managers' portfolios, their trading strategies, and their use of leverage. In the model by Sharpe [91], the focus is on the location component of returns, which reveals the asset categories the manager invests in. Their model extends Sharpe's approach by incorporating factors that reflect how a manager trades. They use factor analysis to extend Sharpe's style analysis to include dynamic trading strategies. They factor analyze 409 hedge funds as a single group and are able to find five mutually orthogonal principal components – System/Opportunistic, Global/Macro, Value, System/Trend following, and Distressed. These five components explain roughly 43% of the cross-sectional return variance, which is an improvement compared to the traditional style analysis.

Agarwal and Naik [3] conduct a generalized return-based style analysis of various hedge fund strategies by relaxing the constraints of the conventional style analysis. They estimate a stepwise regression where they drop an index if they find an insignificant style weight on it. They then re-compute the style weights and their revised standard errors and repeat this procedure until only indices having significant style weights are left in the model. They find that generalized style analysis approach is more robust for estimating risk exposures of hedge funds that take short positions in various asset classes and typically hold significant part of their portfolio in cash. Their sample period runs from January 1994 to September 1998, a period that covers market up and downturns and times of high and low volatility. In order to reveal how the performance of different hedge fund strategies in good and bad times, they report the returns on eight different hedge fund strategies during seven large up moves and seven large down moves of the S&P 500 composite index over the sample period. They find that none of the non-directional strategies are truly market neutral. They gain less than the S&P 500 index during market up-moves but they also lose less than the index during market down-moves. In contrast, the directional strategies tend to move with the market, performing significantly better than the non-directional ones during market upturns and significantly worse during market downturns.

Brown and Goetzmann [28] follow a slightly different quantitative approach based on an extension of k-means cluster analysis to analyze different hedge fund styles. They find at least eight distinct hedge fund styles that lead to differences in risk exposures of hedge funds. Further, they show that differences in investment styles can explain about 20% of the cross-sectional variation in hedge fund returns. Bares, Gibson, and Gyger [20] use another form of clustering methodology, namely fuzzy clustering, to examine style consistency in hedge funds. Maillet and Rousset [82] use a different classification algorithm called Kohonen mapping to classify hedge funds.

2.3. Nonlinear payoff structure of hedge funds

Several studies, for example, Fung and Hsieh [48], Mitchell and Pulvino [85], and Agarwal and Naik [5], have observed a nonlinear relation between hedge fund returns and market returns and proposed more sophisticated methods for studying neutrality. They all claim that hedge funds do have systematic risk but this risk cannot be observed in the context of a linear-factor model applied to standard asset benchmarks. Agarwal and Naik [5] suggest using piecewise linear models for the hedge fund returns as a function of the market return.

They characterize the systematic risk exposures of hedge funds using buy-and-hold and option-based strategies. The option strategy used by Agarwal and Naik [5] involves trading once a month in short-maturity highly liquid European put and call options on the S&P 500 index. On the first trading day in every month, a call or put option on the S&P 500 with a couple of months to maturity is purchased. On the first trading day on the following month, the option is sold and another call or put option on the S&P 500 index that expires in a couple of months is bought. This trading strategy is repeated every month. The returns from this trading strategy are calculated for two options: at-the-money options and out-of-the money options. The results show that a large number of equity-oriented hedge fund strategies exhibit payoffs resembling a short position in a put option on the market. Dor, Jagannathan, and Meier [40] confirm this result.

Agarwal and Naik [5] propose a two-step approach to characterize hedge fund risks. In the first step they estimate the risk exposures of hedge funds using a multifactor model consisting of excess returns on standard assets and options on those assets as risk factors. In the second step they examine the ability of these risk factors to replicate the out-of-sample performance of hedge funds. The out-of-sample analysis confirms that the risk factors estimated in the first step represent underlying economic risk exposures of hedge funds. Assuming that the hedge funds were bearing the same systematic risk exposures as those during the 1990s, Agarwal and Naik [5] estimate the returns prior to the sample period and compare the long-term performance of hedge funds with their performance during the 1990s. They find that the performance during the last decade is not representative of the long-term performance of hedge funds. In particular, the mean returns during the 1927–1989 period, are significantly lower and the standard deviations are significantly higher compared to those of the recent performance.

Agarwal and Naik [5] propose a general model for analyzing hedge fund strategies. However, specific strategies have also been analyzed in the literature using a bottom-up approach of starting with the underlying conventional assets such as stocks and bonds. Fung and Hsieh [48] term this approach as Asset-Based Style (ABS) analysis.

Using this approach, they show theoretically that trend-following strategies can be represented as an option strategy. They demonstrate that the return profile of trend-following strategy indicates that the relationship between trend followers and the equity market is nonlinear. Although returns of trend-following funds have a low beta against equities on average, the state dependent beta estimates tend to be positive in up markets and negative in down markets. Fung and Hsieh [48] posit that the trend-following strategy has a payoff structure similar to that of a look-back straddle.[1] The implication of their results is that trend-following funds have a systematic risk and hence are not market neutral. Fung and Hsieh [49] provide an out-of-sample validation of the findings in Fung and Hsieh [48]. They do this using the four years of data available since the previous paper was published. They find that the model correctly predicted the return behavior of trend-following strategies during out-of-sample periods, in particular during stressful market conditions like those of September 2001. In similar spirit, Fung and Hsieh [51] model convergence trading with options to explain the returns of fixed-income funds. Convergence trading bets on the relative price between two assets to narrow (or converge) so approximately offsetting positions are taken in two securities that have similar, but not identical, characteristics and trade at different prices. Convergence trading is risky, because the relative price of these assets can just as easily diverge. This is particularly so in the case of fixed-income applications of convergence trading. While for stocks the dominant risk factor is the systematic market component, fixed-income securities are subject to several important risk factors, not just the level of interest rates. The convergence trading strategy is basically the opposite of the trend-following strategy. A trend-following strategy tries to capture a large price move, up or down. Typically, the trend-follower observes a trend by waiting for the price of an asset to exceed certain thresholds. When the asset price goes above (below) the given threshold, a long (short) position in the asset is initiated. Assuming the same set of keys are used, the trend-following trader and the convergence trader will

---

[1] The owner of a look-back call option has the right to buy the underlying asset at the lowest price over the life of the option. Similarly, a look-back put option allows the owner to sell at the highest price. The combination of the two options is the look-back straddle.

have similar entry and exit decisions, but in exact opposite directions. In Fung and Hsieh [48], the payoff of trend-following strategies is modeled as a long position in a look-back straddle. Since convergence trading is the opposite of the trend-following strategy, the convergence trading strategy can be modeled as a short position in a look-back straddle.

Another paper that uses an ABS approach is by Mitchell and Pulvino [85], who analyze almost 5000 mergers from 1963 to 1998 to characterize the risk and return in risk arbitrage. Results indicate that risk arbitrage returns have zero correlation with the market during up-market conditions, but large positive correlation during down-market conditions. This suggests that returns to risk arbitrage are similar to those obtained from selling uncovered index put options. In order to examine if this is true for a wide range of hedge fund indices, they use a piecewise regression specification that allows for separate intercept and slope coefficients when the market index is above and below its median return. Using contingent claim analysis that controls for the nonlinear relationship with market returns, and after controlling for transaction costs, they find that risk arbitrage generates returns of 4% per year.

Agarwal, Fung, Loon, and Naik [7] also use ABS approach using data on Japanese and US convertible bonds and underlying stocks to analyze the risk-return characteristics of convertible arbitrage funds. Convertible arbitrage strategy usually involves buying a portfolio of convertible securities and hedging equity risk by short-selling the underlying stock. They hypothesize that there are three primitive trading strategies that explain convertible arbitrage funds' returns. These include positive carry, volatility arbitrage, and credit arbitrage trading strategies. Positive carry strategy is designed to create a delta-neutral portfolio with positive interest income comprising a long position in the convertible bond and a short position in the underlying stock, thereby minimizing equity risk and credit risk. Volatility arbitrage strategy seeks to exploit underpricing in the embedded option in convertible bonds by actively managing a delta-neutral, but long gamma position in the underlying equity whilst minimizing interest rate risk and credit risk. Credit arbitrage strategy is designed to create a long credit spread position while minimizing interest rate risk and equity risk. It is designed to capture value from over/under priced credit risk inherent in the convertible bonds. Following prior literature, they refer to these as asset-based style (ABS) factors. Their empirical analysis shows that these ABS factors can explain a significant proportion of the return variation of four popular convertible arbitrage indices.

Fung and Hsieh [53] use ABS factors to create hedge fund benchmarks that capture the common risk factors in hedge funds. They identify seven risk factors that include two equity factors (equity market and size), two fixed income factors (bond market and credit spread), and three trend-following factors for bond, currency, and commodity markets. Their empirical tests show that these seven risk factors can jointly explain a major proportion of return movements in hedge fund portfolios, using funds of hedge funds as a proxy for hedge fund portfolios. The R-squares range from 55% to 80% depending on what time period is used.

The research presented above all investigates the claim of market neutrality of hedge funds. In general, they find that the return of hedge funds are exposed to systematic risk and have option-like features. The question arises whether this is also true for commodity trading advisors (CTAs). Fung and Hsieh [44] point out that the CTA returns resemble a U-shape, consistent with an option-like return. The CTA portfolio behaves, on average, like a straddle, conditional on the different states of the global equity markets; it pays out the largest amounts during the extreme up and down months. They question is whether these return patterns are likely to persist or if the pattern is just another form of survivorship bias. They answer the question by examining the return of dissolved CTA funds. If dissolved CTA funds do not exhibit a similar return pattern, the option-like features may not persist, because they may be specific to only a small number of surviving CTA funds. However, they find that the pattern is the same for dissolved funds. Hence, CTAs are also exposed to systematic risk and thus are not market neutral.

2.4. Manager skill in hedge funds

The alpha is the return of the hedge fund that cannot be explained by exposure to the systematic risk factors. It is generally interpreted as return attributed to the manager's skills. Many papers claim that most hedge fund groups display positive unexplained returns, which provides evidence of manager skill, see for example, Liang [73]. Fung and Hsieh [52] show empirically that Equity Long/Short hedge funds have significant alpha to both conventional as well as alternative risk factors utilizing hedge fund data from three major databases, Hedge Fund Research (henceforth HFR), TASS, and Morgan Stanley Capital International (MSCI). To identify common risk in Equity Long/Short hedge funds, they regress three indices on Fama-French three-factor model augmented with the momentum factor as implemented by Carhart [33]. In all regressions, the two most important risk factors turn out to be the excess return in the market and the size factor. The book-to-market factor is not statistically significant in any regression and the momentum factor does not add substantial explanatory power beyond the two-factor regression in terms of adjusted R-squares. They also check for evidence of market timing by adding the absolute values of the regressors – excess return on the market returns and the size factor. The additional regressors included to capture timing ability turn out to be statistically insignificant, suggesting lack of any timing ability in Equity Long/Short hedge funds.

Kosowski, Naik, and Teo [70] examine hedge fund returns using the bootstrap methodology, in order to test whether they can be explained by luck alone. Using a comprehensive database combining the four major databases, Center for International Securities and Derivative Markets (henceforth CISDM), HFR, MSCI, and TASS, they model the cross-sectional distribution of alpha estimates (across all funds) with the bootstrap, and then examine the significance of alpha outliers. The bootstrap estimates indicate that the performance of the top hedge funds cannot be attributed to chance alone. This is true even after adjusting for backfill bias and serial correlation. Also, they discover that hedge fund alpha differences between the best and the worst funds persist over horizons of one to four years. However, an investment strategy designed to take advantage of this persistence will run into difficulties as the top hedge funds are often small and effectively closed to new investments.

Fung, Hsieh, Naik, and Ramadorai [54] apply the seven-factor model by Fung and Hsieh [53] on a database of funds of hedge funds constructed by forming a union of three major databases – HFR, TASS, and CISDM. They show that alphas do matter in discerning the quality of different funds of hedge funds. Specifically, they show that funds of hedge funds exhibiting positive and significantly alphas have less survivorship risk than those that do not. They then divide the universe of funds of hedge funds into two sub groups, those that have alphas (the haves) and those that do not have alpha (the have-nots) and compare the return and money-flow characteristics across these two groups. Investigating the time-series behavior of the haves and have-nots, Fung, Hsieh, Naik, and Ramadorai [54] divide the sample into three sub-periods, February 1994 to September 1998 (pre-LTCM), October 1998 to March 2000 (Internet bubble), and April 2000 to December 2004 (the most recent period). The average fund of hedge funds failed to deliver alpha for two of three sub-periods. Extending this analysis to those funds of hedge funds that have alphas (*the haves*) and those that did not (*the have-nots*), the empirical results in this section confirm that *the haves* consistently delivered statistically delivered alpha in all of the three sub-periods whereas *the have-nots* only deliver statistically significant alpha in the second sub-period. However, even for *the haves* that delivered alpha in all three sub-periods, the level of alpha in the third sub-period is lower than that in the first sub-period. Therefore, not only are the alphas time-varying, the results are consistent with the hypothesis that the alphas among *the haves* in the fund of hedge funds sector are shrinking over time. To uncover the sources of time-varying alphas, they perform an analysis of fund of hedge fund alphas along the line of Sharpe [91] and Fung and Hsieh [43] as a function of the hedge fund styles. The results confirm that the supply of alphas from different hedge fund styles appear to be cyclical in that, depending on the market environment, different hedge fund styles are better sources of alpha. In addition, the empirical results do not show any style-timing ability even among the funds of hedge funds in *the haves* group.

Bailey, Li, and Zhang [17] analyze hedge fund performance using the stochastic discount factor (SDF) approach and imposing the arbitrage-free requirement to correctly value the derivatives and dynamic trading strategies used by hedge funds. Using SDFs of many asset pricing models, they evaluate hedge fund portfolios based on style and characteristics. Without the arbitrage-free requirement, pricing errors are relatively small and a few models can explain hedge fund returns. With this requirement, pricing errors are much bigger, and all models fail to price style and volatility portfolios.

2.5. Other interpretations of alpha

All the studies discussed above find evidence of a positive and significant alpha suggesting that hedge fund managers, on average, add value. However, an alternative explanation for any finding of alpha besides manager skills is simply that the models are missing some risk factor and hence are misspecified. Some suggestions of this have been made in the extant literature.

Bondarenko [23] measures the market price of variance risk, where the value of the variance is estimated from prices of traded options. He finds that the variance risk is priced and its risk premium is negative and economically very large. He argues that the variance return is a key determinant in explaining performance of hedge funds. He shows that hedge funds exhibit negative exposure to the variance return, implying that they routinely sell the variance risk. The exposure to the variance risk accounts for a considerable portion of hedge fund average returns. He observes that the hedge fund industry on average earns about 6.5% annually by shorting the variance risk. Hence, when the variance risk is not accounted for, many hedge fund categories appear to deliver superior risk-adjusted returns, i.e. positive and statistically significant alphas. However, after correcting for the variance risk exposure, Bondarenko [23] finds that positive alphas often become negative or statistically insignificant. As a group, hedge funds no longer seem to add value. He concludes that the variance return should be considered as a new risk factor for hedge funds, which are exposed to liquidity and/or credit risks.

Aragon [15] finds a positive, concave relation between the returns and the share restrictions of private investment funds, and shows that previously documented positive alphas can be interpreted as compensation for holding illiquid fund shares. The annual returns on funds with lockup provisions are approximately 4% higher than those for non-lockup funds, and the alphas of funds with the most liquid shares are either negative or insignificant. This paper also finds a positive association between share restrictions and illiquidity in fund assets, suggesting that funds facing high redemption costs use restrictions to screen for investors with low-liquidity needs. The results are consistent with the idea that liquidity is priced, and that less liquid assets are held by investors with longer investment horizon.

It is also possible that the alphas are generated due to the fact that there is no cheap and practical way for individual investors to execute the dynamic strategies involving derivatives that hedge funds implement. Hence, in this context, the alphas of the hedge funds are not due to manager skills, but are attributable to the superior resources available to hedge fund managers, which are not available to individual investors. Thus, even though hedge funds charge high fees, investing through them can greatly improve investors' utility. Results in Ackermann, McEnally, and Ravenscraft [1] seem to support this argument. They find that, on average, hedge funds' ability to earn superior gross returns is almost equal to the incentive and administrative fee charged by them.

2.6. Persistence in the performance of hedge funds

If the superior return of hedge funds is due to manager skill then you would expect to see that the same funds have a high return year after year, that is, that they exhibit persistence in returns. The question arises as to whether hedge funds are able to consistently add value. This is an important issue in the context of hedge funds because, unlike traditional mutual funds, an investment in hedge funds involves significant lock-up period. This implies that the investor needs to have sufficient information about the performance of hedge funds over a long period before committing their money to them. Further, one would expect to see more persistence in hedge fund performance if the managers have more flexibility in their investment strategies arising from greater restrictions on money outflows through longer lockup and redemption periods. Moreover, as hedge funds exhibit a much higher attrition rate compared to mutual funds, the issue of performance persistence becomes especially important in the case of hedge funds. If there is no persistence in hedge fund performance, then the investor may be better off selecting funds based on other fund-specific attributes such as reputation, investment style, and fees.

Using annual data for a sample of offshore hedge funds, Brown, Goetzmann, and Ibbotson [29] find no evidence of persistence. However, they document that the "Specialist Credit" and "Relative Value" strategies dominate the other investment strategies in terms of the proportion of funds that consistently outperform their median peers. Besides, there is no evidence that funds performing better than the median fund are more risky than their peers.

Agarwal and Naik [2], using monthly data, find that hedge fund performance persist, but only for short periods. At the annual horizon, persistence disappears. The same conclusion is reached by Chen [35], who finds support for short-horizon persistence. Agarwal and Naik [2] investigate persistence in the performance of hedge funds using a framework in which the likelihood of observing persistence by chance is lower than in the traditional two-period framework. Under the null hypothesis of no manager skill (no persistence), the theoretical distribution of the observed wins or losses follows binomial distribution. They compare the performance measures in the current period on the performance measures in the previous period. They employ two performance measures: the alpha and the appraisal ratio, with the latter measure being leverage-invariant. They examine whether persistence is sensitive to the length of return measurement intervals by using quarterly, half-yearly, and yearly returns. To investigate the issue of persistence in the two-period framework, they use regression-based (parametric) and contingency-based (non-parametric) methods. For the regression-based parametric method, they regress the alphas (appraisal ratios) during the current period on the alphas during the previous period. A positive significant slope coefficient on a past alpha (appraisal ratio) suggests that a hedge fund that did well in a given period did well in the subsequent period and vice versa. For the non-parametric method, they construct a contingency table of winners and losers where a fund is a winner if the alpha of that fund is greater than the median alpha of all the funds following the same strategy in that period, otherwise it is a loser. This framework is then extended to a multi-period framework. Their results suggest that the extent of persistence decreases as the return measurement interval increases. Whenever persistence is observed, it is mainly attributable to losers continuing being losers. Agarwal and Naik [2] find evidence of a few good managers who consistently outperform their peers over long periods, indicating the importance of manager selection in the context of hedge funds. Both non-directional and directional funds exhibit a similar degree of persistence. The level of persistence based on a multi-period performance measure is considerable smaller than that observed under a two-period framework with virtually no evidence of persistence at the yearly return horizon.

Edwards and Caglayan [41] examine persistence in hedge fund performance during January 1990 to August 1998 period using alphas from a six-factor risk model. They employ both parametric and non-parametric procedures to study persistence over one-year and two-year horizons. They find evidence of significant persistence over these two horizons and document that degree of persistence varies with investment styles. Also, Bares, Gibson, and Gyger [19] investigate the performance persistence of hedge funds over short- and long-term investment horizons. Their methodology differs from the one proposed by Brown, Goetzmann, and Ibbotson [29] and Agarwal and Naik [2] who compare the number of winners and losers and test the significance of the difference form one year or quarter to the next. Here, they rely on non-parametric test to analyze the relative performance persistence of the funds included in the Financial Risk Management database over the period that extends from January 1992 to December 2000. Ranking managers according to their average returns over 1 to 36 months, they form five portfolios that contain the top-performing funds and five others that contain the worst performers. These portfolios are then held for periods extending from 1 to 36 months. They find evidence of short-term persistence which rapidly vanishes as the formation and holding periods lengthen. They also examine whether hedge funds display long-term risk-adjusted performance persistence. They use the Arbitrage Pricing Theory (APT) framework to estimate the hedge fund portfolios' alphas over two independent holding periods. They find existence of a slight reversal in the fund portfolios' alphas over a 36-month holding period. They observe that the "Directional trading", "Traditional", and "Stock Selection" strategies exhibit the greatest tendency to overreact. Finally, the hedge fund portfolios' alphas are very unstable over time. Overall, their findings indicate that investors need to be very cautions when relying on past performance measures to select hedge fund portfolios for long-term investment horizons.

Baquero, Horst, and Verbeek [21] address the issue of high attrition rate in the hedge fund industry and argue that standard persistence tests may be biased if the fund survival depends on historical performance. They propose controlling for the look-ahead bias in tests of persistence. Look-ahead bias arises from conditioning the tests on funds' survival over a period of time. In addition to controlling for look-ahead bias, they control for investment styles and confirm Agarwal and Naik's [2] previous finding of significant short-term persistence over quarterly horizon and less long-term persistence over annual horizon.

Boyson and Cooper [25] do not find any performance persistence in hedge funds, both over short and long horizons, when funds are selected solely on past performance. However, when funds are selected based on past performance and manager tenure, they find persistence over short horizon, i.e., quarterly intervals. They find that less experienced and good past performers consistently outperform their peers. They impose a more stringent requirement for classifying good performance, where funds in the top 10% are considered good, in contrast to the typical classification of top 50% of the funds in a period as good performers. In addition, they control for style effects by including the style indices in a multifactor model and find that there is no persistence even at the quarterly level using these stringent requirements. However, they find persistence at quarterly horizon as found by Agarwal and Naik [2] if they do not control for style indices. They conclude this as evidence of style factors accounting for persistence found in earlier studies.

Koh, Koh, and Teo [69] explore persistence in the performance of hedge funds that mainly invest in Asia. They find that returns of these Asian hedge funds persist most strongly at monthly horizons to quarterly horizons. This persistence weakens considerably when they lengthen the measurement period beyond a quarter, and does not appear to be due to imputation of fees or to systematic risk as measured by a simple factor model.

Kat and Menexe [67] study the persistence and predictability of several statistical parameters of individual hedge fund returns. They find little evidence of persistence in mean returns but do find strong persistence in hedge funds' standard deviations and their correlation with the stock market. Persistence in skewness and kurtosis is low but this could be due to the small size of the sample used. Despite the observed persistence, their study also shows that in absolute terms, hedge funds' risk profiles are not easily predicted from historical returns alone. The true value of a hedge fund's track record therefore appears not to lie in its use as a predictor of future performance and risk, but primarily in the insight that it provides in a fund's risk profile relative to that of other funds in the same strategy group.

2.7. Market timing ability of hedge funds

If hedge fund managers add value, this value addition can come either from security selection ability or from market timing ability. Conflicting evidence of whether hedge funds manager possess market timing ability or not has been found in the academic literature.

Fung, Xu, and Yau [55] examine the performance of 115 global equity-based hedge funds with reference to their target geographical markets in the seven-year period from 1994 to 2000. The results are that global hedge fund managers do not show positive market timing ability but demonstrate superior security-selection ability. Aragon [14] extends the market timing model of Merton [84] to the case of multiple risk factors and derives the equilibrium value of a market timer's forecasting ability. He evaluates the performance of funds of hedge funds and show that, both individually and in aggregate, funds of hedge funds do not exhibit timing ability with respect to a variety of hedge fund styles. He also shows that there is a positive relationship between portfolio liquidity and estimates of market timing ability. Moreover, market timing ability is positive (negative) for funds holding the most liquid (illiquid) portfolios.

Chen [35] examines the timing ability of hedge funds covering various investment categories. He tests if hedge funds time their focus markets, i.e. the markets in which the funds trade most actively among several markets. Using a sample from TASS and HFR databases, he finds evidence of successful market timing at both the category level and at the individual fund level, especially with the convertible arbitrage funds in the high-yield bond market, and the market timing funds in the US equity market.

2.8. Hedge funds and the technology bubble

Given the conflicting evidence on timing ability of hedge fund managers, it is interesting to investigate how hedge fund returns were affected by the technology bubble in the end of the 1990s. Brunnermeier and Nagel [32] examine stock holdings of hedge funds during the time of the technology bubble on NASDAQ and find that the portfolios of these sophisticated investors were heavily tilted towards overpriced technology stocks. This does not seem to be a result of unawareness of the bubble. At an individual stock level, hedge funds reduced their exposure before prices collapsed, and their technology stock holdings outperformed characteristics-matched benchmarks. Their findings do not confirm the efficient markets view of rational speculation, which is based on the assumption that rational speculators find it optimal to attack price bubbles and thus exert a correcting force on prices. Instead, their results are consistent with models in which rational investors can find it optimal to ride bubbles because of predictable investor sentiment and limits to arbitrage.

3

Hedge Fund Characteristics and Performance

Hedge funds are characterized by some unique characteristics such as the managerial compensation structure, managerial flexibility arising from restrictions on capital withdrawals, and co-investing by the manager. In the previous section, we largely reviewed the literature explaining the time-series variation in hedge fund returns. In this section, we review another strand of hedge fund literature that examines the cross-sectional variation in hedge fund returns. This literature investigates the association of different hedge fund characteristics with the performance of hedge funds.

3.1. Compensation and performance

Hedge fund managers are typically compensated using two types of fees – a management fee, which is a fixed percentage of assets under management, and incentive fees, which are related to the fund performance. The incentive fees are usually subject to hurdle rate and high-water mark provisions. Hurdle rate provision implies that the manager only earns the incentive fee if the fund return is above a chosen hurdle rate such as the risk free rate like LIBOR. High-water mark provision states that the manager can earn the incentive fee only if the fund's net asset value (NAV) exceeds its previous maximum. Since the manager participates only in the upside, the incentive fee contract is asymmetric resembling a call option written by the investors on the assets under management, where the strike price is determined by the NAV at which different investors enter the fund, and the hurdle rate and high-water mark provisions. Since capital flows into the fund at different points in time, each flow will have its own strike price. Hence, the incentive fee contract is effectively a portfolio of call options where each option is related to the flow each year having its own strike price. Anson [13] uses the Black–Scholes option pricing model to determine an approximate value of the incentive-fee option for three hedge fund strategies, and find that the option has considerable value. Performance-based incentive fee along with co-investment by manager should address the agency problems and lead to better alignment of interests between the manager and the investors.

Researchers have examined if such incentive alignment mechanisms do indeed result in better hedge fund performance. Ackermann, McEnally, and Ravenscraft [1] study the relation between incentive fee and risk-adjusted performance using Sharpe ratio as the proxy. They find a strong association between incentive fees and Sharpe ratio. An increase in the incentive fees from zero to the median value of 20% leads to an average increase in the Sharpe ratio of 66%. They conclude that incentives are effective at aligning the interests of the manager and the investors as well as in attracting top managers. They do not find a negative relation between management fee and performance, though this relation is mostly insignificant. Liang [73] also conducts a similar cross-sectional analysis of average monthly returns with respect to incentive fees and management fees. He finds a significantly positive slope coefficient for incentive fee to conclude that a high incentive fee is able to align the manager's incentive with fund performance. Further, he finds the management fee is not significantly related to performance, which he claims is not surprising because the management fee charged is independent of performance. Edwards and Caglayan [41] also study the relation between incentive fees and performance. They categorize funds into high-incentive-fee funds (those with incentive fee greater than 20%), moderate-incentive-fee funds (those with incentive fee between 2% and 20%), and low-incentive-fee funds (those with incentive fee lower than 2%). Their results suggest that high-incentive-fee funds earn an annualized excess return of about 3–6% higher than that earned by low-incentive-fee funds. Using data on Asian hedge funds from AsiaHedge and EurekaHedge, Koh, Koh, and Teo [69] find no evidence to suggest that funds with higher expenses (management and performance fees) achieve higher returns. Instead, they find the coefficient on the performance fees is negative and significant at the 10% level. Kouwenberg and Ziemba [71] also find that the average returns, both in absolute and risk-adjusted terms, are significantly lower for funds that charge incentive fees.

All these papers implicitly proxy managerial incentives by the percentage incentive fee charge by the hedge funds. However, the incentive fee does not take into account how far the fund is relative to its high-water mark. With two managers charging the same percentage incentive fee, one may be substantially below its high-water mark while the other may be close to its high-water mark. Since the two managers face very different incentives, it is clear that the incentive fee has limitations in capturing the true incentives faced by a manager. Agarwal, Daniel, and Naik [6] recognize these limitations and propose the use of delta of the hedge fund manager's call-option-like incentive-fee-contract along with hurdle rate and high-water mark provisions, to proxy for managerial incentives. Delta represents the expected dollar increase in the manager's compensation for a 1% increase in the fund's NAV. They find that funds with better managerial incentives (higher delta and presence of high-water mark) do perform better.

3.2. Theoretical models on optimal incentive contracts

Lucas and Siegmann [80] interpret the incentive scheme used in the hedge fund industry as (i) stimulating the manager to maximize expected fund wealth and (ii) making him loss averse to avoid moral hazard problems, i.e. taking excessive risk. By combining the two properties and using the theory of loss aversion as put forward in the behavioral finance literature, they show that the typical manager's incentive schemes give rise to a variety of investment strategies. Which of these strategies is optimal depends on the manager's position with respect to her benchmark return and type of possible investments. They assume that the manager has a loss-averse objective function, where he faces a trade-off between expected return and the expected shortfall below the benchmark return.

Lucas and Siegmann [81] derive the optimal payoffs with one option for an agent with loss averse preferences. A total of four different payoffs are found to be optimal, depending on the strike price of the option and whether the initial position of the agent is one of surplus or shortfall. The shape of the optimal payoffs for an initial shortfall position corresponds either to a short put or short straddle. This can be related to managers that are below their customary return, suggesting that investment strategies creating a short put payoff like those by Long Term Capital Management might be driven by loss-averse preferences. Furthermore, the steepness of the payoffs under loss aversion increases in the difference to an initial reference point, which corresponds to hedge funds increasing their risk when performance falls further behind.

Goetzmann, Ingersoll, and Ross [60] provide a closed-form solution to the high-water mark contract under certain conditions and show that managers have an incentive to take risks. They show analytically that the value of the manager's contract is increasing in portfolio variance due to the call option-like feature of the incentive contract. With their model they find that the present value of fees and other cost could be as high as 33% of the amount invested. A significant proportion of this compensation is due to the incentive feature of the contract; however, the trade-off between regular fees and high-water mark fees depends upon the volatility of the portfolio and the investor's withdrawal policy. They find that this proportion is high when the probability of investors leaving the fund is high, and when the volatility of the assets is high. In contrast, when investors are likely to remain for the long term, and when the volatility is low, the regular-fee portion of the contract provides the greatest value to the manager.

Panageas and Westerfield [88] also study the optimal portfolio choice of hedge fund managers who are compensated by high-water mark contracts. They find that even risk-neutral managers will not place unboundedly large weights on risky assets. The intuition given for the results are the following. A bolder portfolio today could help overcome the high-water mark more quickly, but it will also increase the likelihood that next period, the manager has to start far below the threshold. Bolder portfolios reduce the mean logarithmic growth rate of wealth after a certain point. Therefore, even though portfolio variance helps to attain the goal of overcoming the previously recorded high-water mark, it comes at the cost of reducing the mean growth rate of wealth. A hedge fund manager considers the trade-off between the two effects, and the desire to maximize expected discounted compensation fees will lead the manager to exploit opportunities as if he exhibited constant relative risk aversion.

3.3. Managerial flexibility and performance

Hedge funds usually impose significant restrictions on capital withdrawals in the form of lockup, redemption, and notice periods. These impediments allow the manager to greater freedom to pursue different investment strategies. For example, managers may invest in arbitrage opportunities that may take time to become profitable due to noise trader risk or managers may not be forced to unwind their positions during unfavorable market conditions. Extant literature argues that such flexibility should be associated with better performance. Liang [73] documents a positive relation between lockup period and average fund returns. He argues that longer lockup periods may result in lower cash holdings and investment from long-term point of view, resulting in better performance. Koh, Koh, and Teo [69] also find that funds with higher redemption periods achieve higher returns on average due to their ability to extricate from their positions in a timely fashion in the face of redemptions. Agarwal, Daniel, and Naik [6] show that funds with greater managerial flexibility manifested through greater impediments to capital withdrawals in form of longer lockup and redemption periods, are associated with better future performance. This is consistent with investors earning a liquidity premium, an argument also made by Aragon [15] discussed earlier in this review.

3.4. Fund size and performance

Liang [73] finds the coefficient on assets under management to be significantly positive indicating that larger funds have better performance. He attributes this finding to larger funds having economies of scale or attracting more money. Koh, Koh, and Teo [69] document a positive relationship in a univariate setting between firm size and fund returns which is consistent with the economies of scale argument. However, this effect goes away in a multivariate setting. Hence, both Liang [73] and Koh, Koh, and Teo [69] document a positive relationship between size and performance. Studying the relationship between size and performance can have two different implications. For the investor, it involves taking the size of the fund into account before investing. For the fund manager, it raises the issue of optimal size to be decided upon. Getmansky [56] find a concave relationship between performance and assets under management. The implication of this study is that an optimal asset size can be obtained by balancing out the effects of past returns, fund flows, market impact, competition and favorable category positioning that are modeled in the paper. Hedge funds in illiquid categories are subject to high market impact, have limited investment opportunities, and are more likely to exhibit an optimal size behavior compared to those in more liquid hedge fund categories. Finally, Agarwal, Daniel, and Naik [6] examine the impact of both fund size and investors' money flows on the performance of hedge funds. They find that both larger hedge funds as well as funds experiencing greater flows are associated with worse future performance. This finding is consistent with hedge funds facing decreasing returns to scale.

3.5. Fund age, manager tenure, and performance

Liang [73] finds the age of the fund to be negatively related to average performance. Long-lived funds do not necessarily outperform short-lived funds in the sample. One explanation put forward is that managers of young funds work harder at building up reputation. While Liang [73] finds a negative relationship between age and performance, Koh, Koh, and Teo [69] could not verify that relationship for Asian funds.

Howell [65] investigates the relationship between the age of hedge funds and their performance, from 1994 to 2000. Young hedge funds are defined as those with a track record of less than three years. Ex-ante returns infer that young funds' returns are superior to those of seasoned funds: the youngest decile exhibits a return of 21.5%, while the whole sample median exhibits a return of 13.9%. He concludes that hedge fund performance deteriorates over time, even when the risk of failure is taken into account. Boyson [24] analyses the relationship between hedge fund manager tenure and performance. As far as the manager tenure is concerned, regressions show that each additional year of experience is associated with a statistically significant decrease in the annual returns of approximately -0.8%. The negative relationship between experience and performance is explained in the light of risk-taking behavior. The sources of hedge fund manager's compensation are the assets under management and the returns. Young managers generally have a lower level of assets under management than older managers. Consequently, they take more risk to obtain good returns, while the large size of the fund provides older managers with their compensation. As a result, the risk level diminishes as the hedge fund manager's age rises. Moreover, statistics show that failed hedge fund managers rarely start a new hedge fund, and if they move into the mutual fund industry, for example, this is associated with a pay cut. The amount of the pay cut is more significant for older hedge fund managers, and it is thus an incentive for them to mitigate their risk-taking behavior. A final explanation put forward for the lower level of risk taken by an older hedge fund manager is the large amount of personal assets invested in the fund.

3.6. Hedge fund style and performance

Brown and Goetzmann [28] study the relationship between hedge fund style and performance. Are there a few basic styles that hedge funds pursue and do these styles explain differences in performance? They find eight dominant styles that explain about 20% of the cross-sectional variability of fund returns. These styles include US equity hedge, event driven, global macro, pure emerging market, non-US equity hedge, non-directional/relative value, pure leveraged currency, and pure property. They find that risk exposures depend on style affiliation. They also find that the persistence of fund returns from year to year has a lot to do with the particular style of fund management.

Having reviewed the literature on the relation between various hedge fund characteristics and performance, in the following section, we summarize the research relating some of these characteristics to the risk-taking behavior of hedge fund managers.

4

Hedge Fund Characteristics and Risk-Taking Behavior

4.1. Compensation and risk-taking behavior of hedge fund managers

As discussed earlier, the incentive fee contract of hedge fund managers is an effectively a portfolio of call options. Managers can increase the value of this portfolio of options by increasing the volatility of their fund. The holder of a call option (here the fund manager) will prefer more variance in the price of the underlying asset because the greater the variance, the greater the probability that the asset value will exceed the strike price. Investors in the hedge fund own the underlying partnership units, and receive payoffs offered by the entire distribution of return outcomes. They are generally risk averse and dislike higher volatility. Whether hedge fund managers have a tendency to increase the volatility of the fund due to the nature of the incentive fee contract has been examined in a number of papers.

Although the incentive-fee contract is asymmetric and does not explicitly penalize poorly performing managers, there are great implicit costs to taking risks that might lead to termination. Fung and Hsieh [44] show that reputational concerns and contractual constraints may mitigate or prevent managers to increase variance when the incentive contract is out of the money. They argue that there is a clear tension between risk taking and the desire to develop or preserve a reputation once the reputation has been developed. Brown, Goetzmann, and Park [31] investigate the volatility of hedge funds and CTAs in light of managerial career concerns. The contract provisions for hedge fund managers and CTAs would suggest that they have a strong incentive to take on extreme risk, particular when their incentive contract is out-of-the-money. However, excess premia and poor relative performance increase the probability of termination, and this represents a reputation cost sufficient to offset the adverse risk-taking incentives created by the incentive fee contract. They find that hedge fund risks depend on relative performance with the better performing funds reducing their risk and limited evidence on poorly performing managers taking more risks. The fact that variance strategies depend on relative but not absolute performance suggests that reputation costs indeed play a significant role in modifying incentives to take risk. Using a behavioral framework of prospect theory, Kouwenberg and Ziemba [71] find that hedge funds with incentive-fee-contract are not significantly more risky than the funds without such a contract. Using certain parameter values in their theoretical model, they document that the risk-taking behavior is dampened significantly when the manager invests substantial amount of his own money (more than 30%) into the fund. It should be noted that the data on manager's investment in the fund is not available to empirically test its impact on the risk-taking behavior of managers. Even if such data was available, it would be more appropriate to use the level of manager's investment as a fraction of his wealth to capture the risk-aversion induced by co-investment.

4.2. Hedge fund characteristics and survival

Getmansky [56] analyzes the life cycles of hedge funds. Using the TASS database, she studies industry-specific and fund-specific factors that affect the survival probability of hedge funds. Her findings show that, in general, investors chasing fund performance decrease probabilities of hedge funds liquidating. However, if investors follow a category of hedge funds that has performed well, then the probability of hedge funds liquidating in this category increases. She interprets this finding as a result of competition among hedge funds in a category. As competition increases, marginal funds are more likely to be liquidated than funds that deliver superior risk-adjusted returns.

5

Funds of Hedge Funds

A problem to the investors is the high degree of fund-specific risk and the lack of transparency in hedge funds. In addition, many of the most attractive hedge funds are closed to new investment. Funds of hedge funds resolve these issues by providing investors with diversification across manager styles and professional oversight of fund operations that can provide the necessary degree of due diligence. In addition, many funds of hedge funds hold shares in hedge funds otherwise closed to new investment allowing smaller investors to access the most sought-after managers. Brown, Goetzmann, and Liang [30], however, find that the diversification, oversight, and access come at the cost of a multiplication of the fees paid by the investor. They discover that individual hedge funds dominate funds of hedge funds on an after-fee return or on a Sharpe ratio basis. Hence, the information advantage of funds of hedge funds does not compensate investors for the fees. The same conclusion is found in Amin and Kat [12] where the average stand-alone fund of hedge funds' efficiency loss exceeds that of the average non-fund of funds hedge fund index by 5.17%.

Liang [76] studies hedge funds, funds of hedge funds, and CTAs by investigating their performance, risk, and fund characteristics. Considering them as three distinctive investment classes, he studies them not only on stand-alone basis but also on a portfolio basis. He finds that CTAs differ from hedge funds and funds of hedge funds in terms of trading strategies, liquidity, and correlation structures. Second, during 1994–2001, hedge funds outperformed funds of hedge funds, which in turn outperformed CTAs on a stand-alone basis. These results can be explained by the double fee structure but not by survivorship bias. Third, correlation structures for alternative investment vehicles are different under different market conditions. Hedge funds are highly correlated with each other and are not well hedged in the down markets with liquidity squeeze. The negative correlations with other instruments make CTAs suitable hedging instruments for insuring downside risk. When adding CTAs to the hedge fund portfolio or the funds of hedge funds portfolio, investors can benefit significantly from the risk-return trade-off.

6

Hedge Fund Indices

The most common argument made in favor of using hedge fund indices is diversification. The hedge fund index is viewed as an attractive mechanism for diversifying returns. Investing in a hedge fund index is looked on as a means for reducing the overall volatility of a traditional equity and bond portfolio without sacrificing expected returns. Hedge fund indices are constructed to represent the broad hedge fund market. Liew [77] find that a hedge fund index that includes a large fraction of unskilled managers will be significantly worse than a portfolio of actively picked good hedge funds. The paper also suggests that the expected diversification benefits are illusory, and disappear under extreme market conditions. Brooks and Kat [26] demonstrate that although hedge fund indices are highly attractive in mean-variance terms, this is much less the case when skewness, kurtosis, and autocorrelation are taken into account. Sharpe ratios will substantially overestimate the true risk-return performance of portfolios containing hedge funds. Similarly, mean-variance portfolio analysis will over-allocate to hedge funds and overestimate the attainable benefits from including hedge funds in an investment portfolio. They also find substantial differences between indices that aim to cover the same type of strategy.

Investor's perceptions of hedge fund performance and value added will therefore strongly depend on the indices used.

7

Determinants of Investors' Money Flows into Hedge Funds

Hedge funds differ from traditional asset management vehicles in several important ways and one expects these differences to also influence the investors' hedge fund selection process. While much research has been done on the factors that investors consider before placing their money in mutual funds, pension funds, private equity funds, relatively little research has been done on the determinants of money-flows in hedge funds.

Goetzmann, Ingersoll, and Ross [60] investigate this issue for hedge funds by conducting a univariate analysis of money-flows and past returns. Agarwal, Daniel, and Naik [6] examine how money-flows relate to a fund's managerial ability, managerial incentives, and managerial flexibility. They find that money-flows chase returns and are significantly higher (lower) for funds that are persistent winners (losers). This is consistent with funds with higher managerial ability, i.e., better and consistent performance in the past, attracting higher flows. Further, they document that funds with greater managerial incentives experience more flows, suggesting that investors reward funds where there is better alignment of interests between the manager and the investors. Finally, they also find that funds with higher managerial flexibility, i.e., funds with greater restrictions on capital withdrawals, attract less money flows, indicating that everything else equal, investors do not like this illiquidity.

In a recent working paper, Naik, Stromqvist and Ramadorai [87] take the observed capital allocated to different hedge fund strategies over time and examine which finance theoretic predictions come closest to explaining the observed portfolio allocation of the representative hedge fund investor. For example, the investor could use the Markowitz mean-variance efficient portfolio approach; the Bayes-Stein shrinkage portfolio approach; or any of the 'data-and-model' approaches. Alternatively, the investor could simply be using rules of thumb – along the lines of some of the by now well-known behavioural finance models. The authors try to characterize the actual investment behavior of hedge fund investors by comparing the observed capital allocation to different hedge fund strategies with the predictions of various finance theories.

8

Risk Management in Hedge Funds

It is well known that the returns of hedge funds are not normally distributed since they exhibit a negative skewness and large kurtosis. This involves important implications for the risk management of hedge funds.

8.1. Risk management and Value-at-Risk (VaR)

Lo [79] argues that risk management and risk transparency are essential for hedge fund investors. He provides an excellent overview of the aspects of risk management for hedge funds and proposes a set of risk analytics for hedge fund investments. He claims that the ultimate goal is to creating risk transparency without compromising the proprietary nature of hedge fund investment strategies. He argues that the standard risk management tools such as mean-variance analysis, beta, and Value-at-Risk (VaR) do not capture the hedge fund risks appropriately. Alexander and Baptista [8] point out that there are several problems associated with VaR. For example, a portfolio with two securities may be larger than the sum of the VaR of each of the securities in the portfolio. Moreover, using VaR as a measure of risk may lead an agent to increase her exposure to risky assets. For those reasons, they propose the use of Conditional-VaR (CVaR). Both models require a fixed confidence level and an investment horizon. While a portfolio's VaR is the maximum loss one expects to suffer at that confidence level by holding the portfolio over that time horizon, a portfolio's CVaR is the loss one expects to suffer given that the loss is equal to or larger than the portfolio's VaR. They show that the CVaR constraint is more effective than a VaR constraint as a tool to control aggressive fund managers.

Building on these insights, Agarwal and Naik [5] uncover that equity-oriented hedge fund strategies exhibit payoffs resembling a short position in a put option on the market and therefore bear significant left-tail risk, risk that is ignored by the mean-variance framework. They show that the Conditional Value-at-Risk (CVaR) framework, which explicitly accounts for the negative tail risk, can be applied to construct portfolios involving hedge funds.

They demonstrate to what extent the mean-variance framework underestimates the tail risk by using Mean-Conditional Value-at-Risk (M-CVaR). The average ratio of CVaR of mean-variance and M-CVaR efficient portfolios ranges from 1.12 at 90% confidence level to 1.54 at 99% confidence level. This suggests that ignoring the tail risk of hedge funds can result in significantly higher losses during large market downturns.

Gupta and Liang [63] examine the risk characteristics and capital adequacy of nearly 1500 hedge funds. Using VaR-based capital adequacy measures, they find that the majority of hedge funds in the sample are adequately capitalized, with only a small proportion (3.7%) of live funds being undercapitalized. Moreover, all the undercapitalized live funds are relatively small, constituting a small fraction (1.2%) of the total fund assets in the sample. However, amongst dead funds, they find almost 11% to be undercapitalized, which is significantly higher than the percentage of undercapitalized among live funds. This confirms that one of the reasons that funds die is lack of adequate capital. They show that VaR-based measures are superior to traditional risk measures, like standard deviation of returns and leverage ratios, in capturing hedge fund risk. They argue that normality-based standard deviation measures understate the risk and are inappropriate for hedge funds, since their returns exhibit significantly high kurtosis. Also, leverage ratios do not effectively capture hedge fund risk since they are noisy indicators of credit risk to debt holders and ignore the inherent riskiness of the asset portfolios completely. They conclude that Value-at-Risk is effective in capturing the underlying risk trends in hedge fund returns that lead to a fund's death. They find a significant upward trend in VaR for dead funds starting two years before their death, while no such trend is observed for live funds. However, Gupta and Liang [63] acknowledge that VaR estimates are subject to several limitations. First, the historical data may not include representative events for the future. Second, the risk profile of a hedge fund may change more rapidly than what the VaR analysis can capture. Third, the liquidity aspect of hedge fund risk is been ignored in this analysis.

Bali, Gokcan, and Liang [18] propose a theoretical framework that implies a positive relation between VaR and the cross-section of expected returns for loss-averse investors. Using two hedge fund databases from HFR and TASS, they test the empirical validity of the theoretical model by analyzing the cross sectional relationship between VaR and expected return with and without controlling for age, size and liquidity factors. First, based on sorting the estimated VaR, they form 10 portfolios for the live funds and find that the high VaR portfolio outperforms the low VaR portfolio by 9% per annum during the period from January 1995 to December 2003. Investors who buy the high VaR portfolio while short selling the low VaR portfolio can realize a 9% gain on a annual basis. The results provide support for the existence of a relation between downside risk and expected return on hedge funds. Second, the above risk-return relationship is reversed for defunct funds: the higher the VaR the lower the expected return.

Monteiro [86] finds that the critical decision in selecting VaR model for hedge funds is the distributional assumption. In contrast with traditional assets for which the normal distribution presents the best performance, the t-student and the Cornish-Fisher expansion distributional assumptions offer the best performance for hedge funds.

The 1998 failure of Long Term Capital Management (LTCM) is said to have nearly blown up the world's financial system. LTCM held extremely risky positions, magnified by an abnormal 50:1 leverage ratio, thus putting the fund capital at significant risk. Jorion [66] analyzes

LTCM's strategies in terms of the fund's VaR and the amount of capital necessary to support its risk profile. The paper shows that LTCM had severely underestimated its risk due to its reliance on short-term history and risk concentration. He points out that LTCM provides a good example of risk management taken to the extreme. Using the same covariance matrix to measure risk and to optimize positions inevitably leads to biases in the measurement of risk. This approach also induces the strategy to take positions that appear to generate arbitrage profits based on recent history but also represent bets on extreme events, like selling options.

9

Systemic Risks from Hedge Fund Activity

In 1997, after the famous attack on Sterling by George Soros's funds in 1992 and given the current Asian Currency Crisis, regulators took an active interest in hedge fund activities. The IMF initiated a study of the impact of hedge funds on financial markets which resulted in the study by Eichengreen and Mathieson [42]. This study provides information on the activities of hedge funds and analyzed the policy implications with particular reference to the issue of market impact of hedge funds. A major difficulty with this kind of study is the fact that hedge fund positions are difficult to obtain. Except for very large positions in certain futures contracts, foreign currencies, US Treasuries and public equities, hedge funds are not obligated to and generally do not report positions to regulators. Eichengreen and Mathieson [42] resolve this problem by interviewing market participants to obtain estimates of hedge fund positions. In particular, their study analyzes three scenarios:

- use of leverage by a single hedge fund or a small group of hedge funds that can singularly overwhelm a small market,

- herding by other large investors following the lead of a few hedge funds that can overwhelm a market, and

- use of positive feedback trading rules by hedge funds that can amplify a market move.

Their study concludes that there is little reason to believe that hedge funds are more likely to overwhelm a market than other large traders. In their study, the largest single hedge fund has less than USD 10 billion of assets under management and hedge funds as a group has only USD 100–200 billion of capital. This is small compared to the risk capital available to other large investors such as commercial banks, investment banks, insurance companies and corporations. Hence, they conclude that hedge funds are no more likely or able to manipulate a market than any of these entities. Their study also argues that hedge funds are less likely to herd other investors. This is because hedge funds typically view their trading strategies as proprietary and take great pain to prevent disclosure of their positions. Finally, they find no evidence that hedge funds use positive feedback trading strategies.

Fung and Hsieh [46] also provide quantitative estimates on the market impact of hedge funds over a comprehensive set of market events, from the October 1987 stock market crash to the Asian Currency crisis of 1997. They rely on empirical techniques to estimate hedge fund exposures using their performance data. The purpose is to study the same three scenarios as in Eichengreen and Mathieson [42]. Various market events covered by Fung and Hsieh [46] include October 1987 stock market crash, 1992 European Rate Mechanism crisis, 1993 European bond market rally, 1994 European bond market turbulence, 1994–1995 Mexican crisis, and 1997 Asian Currency crisis. In conclusion, they find several periods in which hedge funds activities are prominent and probably exerted market impact. These episodes include the European Rate Mechanism crisis in 1992, the European bond market rally in 1993 and decline in 1994. There are also other episodes in which hedge funds are unlikely to have exerted influence on markets. These include the 1987 stock market crash, the Mexican Peso crisis, and the Asian crisis. Fung and Hsieh [46] find no evidence that hedge funds are able to manipulate markets away from their natural paths driven by economic fundamentals. Further, they find no evidence that hedge funds used positive feedback trading in any of these periods. They also find that hedge funds did not act as a single group and that there is no evidence that hedge funds deliberately herd other investors by executing the same trade.

Chan, Getmansky, Haas, and Lo [34] argue that risk exposures of hedge funds can have a substantial impact on the banking sector resulting in new sources of systemic risk. Using various risk measures including illiquidity risk exposure, nonlinear factor models, liquidation probabilities, and volatility and distress measures using regime-switching models, they document that expected returns of hedge funds are likely to be lower in the future and that systemic risk is likely to increase in the future.

10

Diversification

The issue of diversification comes in two forms. First, with traditional investment vehicles it is known that increasing the number of assets in the portfolio will result in a smaller risk while maintaining the level of expected return. Usually, about fifteen assets are required to achieve good diversification.[1] The question is whether this is also true for hedge funds? Second, given the often low betas with the market, hedge funds are obvious means for investor diversification. Ackermann, McEnally, and Ravenscraft [1] suggest that the low beta values on hedge funds make them a potentially valuable addition to many investors' portfolios. The potential benefits of diversification in the context of hedge funds have been investigated in a number of papers. However, one has to be careful in making a case for hedge funds based only on low correlation. What is important is the extent and significance of improvement in the efficient frontier by addition of hedge funds in a portfolio.

---

[1] See Bodie, Kane, and Marcus [22].

10.1. Increasing the number of hedge funds in a portfolio

The approach in Lhabitant and Learned [72] relies on naive diversification strategies, where they build equally-weighted portfolios of randomly selected hedge funds. By repeating the process several times and studying the characteristics of the resulting portfolios, they are able to study the impact of naively increasing the number of hedge funds in a portfolio. First, they demonstrate that diversification works well in a mean-variance space. That is, increasing the number of hedge funds in a hedge fund portfolio decreases the portfolio's volatility while maintaining its average return level. Further, downside risk is also reduced in a larger-sized hedge fund portfolio. This seems to somewhat validate the existence of funds of hedge funds as useful investment vehicles. However, when they go beyond the mean-variance framework and consider additional factors such as skewness and kurtosis, diversification benefits are reduced. For several strategies, diversification reduces positive skewness, may even generate negative skewness, and increase kurtosis, i.e. there is a trade-off between profit potential and reduced probability of loss. In addition, the correlation with the S&P 500 of large-sized hedge fund portfolios increases, suggesting the danger of attempting to incorporate an unwieldy number of hedge funds in the portfolio construction process. Since most of the diversification benefits are reached for small size portfolios (typically five to ten hedge funds), they conclude that hedge fund portfolios should be cautious on the allocation past this number of funds.

Using monthly return data over the period June 1994 to May 2001, Amin and Kat [9] investigate the performance of randomly selected baskets of hedge funds ranging in size from one to twenty funds. They discover the same findings as in Lhabitant and Learned [72]. Increasing the number of funds can be expected to lead not only to a lower standard deviation but also to lower skewness and increased correlation with the stock market. Most of the change occurs for relatively small portfolios. Holding more than fifteen funds changes little. With fifteen funds however, they still find a substantial degree of variation in performance between baskets, which dissolves only slowly when the number of funds is increased.

Davies, Kat, and Lu [38] provide a method to predict how the higher order return properties of a single-strategy fund of hedge funds will vary as one more fund is added to, or removed from the portfolio. The model-free approach uses average co-moments of hedge funds to develop a functional relationship between portfolio return distributions and the number of funds in the portfolio. They show that some single-strategy funds of hedge funds may be under-diversified and that covariance, co-skewness and co-kurtosis, rather than variance, skewness, and kurtosis matter most in portfolio diversification.

10.2. Mixing hedge funds with a portfolio of traditional investments

Amin and Kat [12] find that the main attraction of hedge funds lies in the weak relationship between hedge fund returns and the returns on other asset classes. As a stand-alone investment, hedge funds do not offer a superior risk-return profile. However, they find that hedge funds classified as inefficient on a stand-alone basis are capable of producing an efficient payoff profile when mixed with the S&P 500. The best results are obtained when 10–20% of the portfolio value is invested in hedge funds. This is in line with the conclusion in Schneeweis and Spurgin [90] who also document that an allocation of between 10 and 20% to alternative investments is appropriate on the basis of the low correlation and improvements in Sharpe ratio. Davies, Kat, and Lu [37] find that the addition of stocks and bonds results in optimal portfolios with less kurtosis and higher skewness when compared with the corresponding optimal portfolios of only hedge funds. In optimal portfolios of stocks, bonds, and hedge funds, equity market neutral funds and global macro funds are imperfect substitutes for bonds.

Hagelin and Promberg [64] examine the returns and investment policies for portfolios of stocks and bonds with and without hedge funds. They apply discrete-time dynamic investment model that allows for all moments of the return distribution to affect the analysis. They find that the gains from adding hedge funds to portfolios of stocks and bonds are statistically significant for most of the strategies involved. Further, hedge funds enter the risk-neutral portfolio as well as the most risk-averse portfolio. Finally, allocations to hedge funds are extensive at times.

Amin and Kat [10] study the diversification effects from introducing hedge funds into a traditional portfolio of stocks and bonds. The results make it clear that in terms of skewness and kurtosis equity and hedge funds do not combine very well. Although the inclusion of hedge funds may significantly improve a portfolio's mean-variance characteristics, it can also be expected to lead to significantly lower skewness as well as higher kurtosis. This means that the case for hedge funds includes a definite trade-off between profit and loss potential. The results also emphasize that to have at least some impact on the overall portfolio, investors will have to make an allocation to hedge funds which by far exceeds the typical 1–5% that many institutions are currently considering.

A theoretical paper by Cvitanic, Lazrak, Martellini, and Zapatero [36] consider the problem of an investor who can choose between the risk-free security and two risky securities: a passive fund that tracks the market and a hedge fund. The hedge fund might offer a positive abnormal expected return or alpha. The investor has power utility and is uncertain about both the expected return of the index and the alpha of the hedge fund, but upgrades beliefs in a Bayesian way. They derive analytic expressions for the optimal investment policy of the investor and calibrate the model to a database of hedge funds.

10.3. Optimal hedge fund portfolio

There are some papers that have approached the question on how to construct an optimal portfolio of hedge funds. One of these is by Giamouridis and Vrontos [59], which uses a full-factor multivariate GARCH model to capture the time-varying nature of hedge fund returns variances and covariances and construct mean-variance and mean-CVaR optimal portfolios. They compare their results with portfolios created in the standard mean-variance and mean-CVaR frameworks where the variances and covariances are constant through time. Their results suggest that the cumulative out-of-sample returns of optimal portfolios constructed with the full-factor multivariate GARCH specification are higher than the cumulative returns of portfolios constructed with the static covariance matrix either in the mean-variance or mean-CVaR framework. When they standardize the out-of-sample returns with the risk undertaken at the time the portfolio construction, the superiority of the full-factor multivariate GARCH specification is more intense. They also find that the CVaR of portfolios constructed in the mean-CVaR framework with the static covariance matrix is higher than the CVaR of the mean-variance portfolios created with the dynamic covariance matrix suggesting that the empirical and the normal distribution assumptions coupled with the static covariance matrix underestimate the tail risk.

Davies, Kat, and Lu [37] incorporate investor preferences into a polynomial goal programming optimization function. The authors solve for multiple competing hedge fund allocation objectives within the mean-variance-skewness-kurtosis framework and show how changing investor preferences can lead to different asset allocation decisions across hedge fund strategies. Their objective function maximizes first and third moments (expected return and skewness) while minimizing the second and fourth moments (standard deviation and kurtosis) simultaneously. This is done with respect to non-negative investor-specific parameters, which represent the investor's subjective degree of preferences for moments. The more importance investors attach to a certain moment (i.e. the greater the preference parameter for this moment), the more favorable the value of this moment statistic is in the optimal portfolio. Comparing with the case of the mean-variance efficient portfolio, if investor preferences over skewness and kurtosis are incorporated into the investor's portfolio decision, then the optimal portfolio may lie below the efficient frontier in mean-variance space. This is because the improvement of portfolio's expected return is not restricted by the simultaneous requirement of improvement of portfolio's skewness and kurtosis. Thus, expected return, skewness and kurtosis are conflicting objectives in portfolio diversification: risk-averse investors reward portfolios with high skewness and low kurtosis with a lower required return. Optimal portfolios in mean-variance space have worse skewness and kurtosis characteristics than optimal portfolios formed within the four-moment framework. Thus, portfolios selected under the traditional mean-variance framework are not the same, and may be strictly inferior, to those selected under a four-moment framework.

One of the limitations of this analysis is that the choices of different sets of relative preferences are not motivated. Some of the sets are not based on reasonable assumptions. For example, in one set the investor only cares about minimizing kurtosis. It is not reasonable to assume that an investor does not care at all about expected return. Also, if the investor only has preference for one moment, you do not need to optimize since you could just rank the hedge funds over that moment. Given that the relative preferences between the four moments can be put into a sensible behavioral context of a sophisticated investor, such as an institutional investor or a fund of hedge fund manager, maximizing over the four moments would make a good allocation model for hedge funds.

11

Biases

Given that hedge fund managers are not required to report data on their performance, there are some natural biases in all hedge fund databases. One of the challenges in academic research on hedge funds is to take into account the various biases in the databases and interpret the results in light of these biases. They include self-selection bias, instant history or backfilling bias, survivorship bias, stale price bias, and multi-period sampling bias. Hedge fund databases can potentially suffer from several of these biases, which can have a significant impact on the performance measures.

11.1. Databases

Before discussing about various biases in the hedge fund databases, here is a non-exhaustive list of databases (with the website links) that have been used in different academic studies on hedge funds:

- Center for International Securities and Derivatives Markets (CISDM) (formerly Zurich Capital Markets and Managed Account Reports) – <http://cisdm.som.umass.edu/ resources/database.shtml>

- Eurekahedge – <http://eurekahedge.com/>

- Hedge Fund Research (HFR) – <http://hedgefundresearch.com/>

- Lipper TASS (formerly TASS) – <http://www.lipperweb.com/products/tass.asp>

- Morgan Stanley Capital International (MSCI) – <http://www.msci.com/hedge/index.html>

- US Offshore Funds Directory – <http://www.hedgefundnews.com/>

- Vanhedge – <http://vanhedge.com/>

In addition, Standard and Poor's provides data on investable hedge fund indices available at <www.sp-hedgefundindex.com>. Most of these databases are publicly available and can be subscribed to at a subsidized rate for academic research.

11.2. Data accuracy and auditing

The choice of an accurate database is of major interest in the context of the hedge fund industry, where a lack of transparency is often observed. Liang [75] focuses on this point. He investigates data accuracy for hedge funds and explores reasons for discrepancies in fund returns across different data sources. The study compares the same funds that appear in two different databases for return discrepancies, TASS and US Offshore Fund Directory. It also analyzes fund returns in TASS database but from two different versions: a previous version and an updated version. Comparison between onshore funds and equivalent offshore funds to see if there are return discrepancies between the two is also performed. Liang [75] finds various factors that have an effect on the quality of the database. These include auditing effectiveness, transparency, verification of funds' returns, and ease of calculating the returns.

The findings are as follows. First, audited funds have much smaller return discrepancies than non-audited funds. Auditing makes a clear difference in data quality. However, over 40% of the hedge funds in their sample are not effectively audited, i.e., they do not have clear auditing dates. Also, there is no increasing trend for funds to be audited. Given the strong correlation between auditing and data accuracy, he strongly recommends that hedge funds be audited and that investors look for audited funds instead of non-audited ones. Second, defunct funds have been less effectively audited than live funds. This may be caused by poor data quality of funds with missing information or by poor administration. Third, there is a significantly positive correlation between the auditing dummy variable and fund size. Large funds tend to be audited, while small funds tend not to be. It is concluded that this is probably because large funds can afford to hire an auditor, and there is more need to audit their large money pools or complicated portfolio positions. Since large funds are more likely to be audited, their data quality is better than data quality for smaller funds. Fourth, funds listed on exchanges, funds of hedge funds, funds with both US and non-US investors, funds open to the public, funds invested in a single sector, and funds that do not use leverage have better data quality than others. It is possible that managers of funds of hedge funds, those listed on exchanges, and those open to the public have carried out due diligence to better keep their books and to report return information more accurately. Their returns also may be more easily calculated, because they do not use leverage and invest only in a single industrial sector.

11.3. Measurement bias

It is well known that the pro forma performance of a sample of investment funds contains biases. The organization structure of hedge funds, as private and often offshore vehicles, makes data collection a much more difficult task, amplifying the impact of performance measurement biases.

Fung and Hsieh [47] focus on the question of performance measurement. They review the biases in hedge fund databases and propose using funds of hedge funds to measure aggregate hedge fund performance, based on the idea that the investment experience of hedge fund investors can be used to estimate the performance of hedge funds. They point out that although the alternative of funds of hedge funds is simple and readily available, there is one problem. The return of funds of hedge funds is a measure of the return on hedge funds net of all costs, including those incurred in managing a portfolio of hedge funds. In all, they find that estimates of the industry's performance statistics, after adjusting for various measurement biases, are consistent with the performance statistics of funds of hedge funds.

Fung and Hsieh [50] make similar arguments, where they discuss the information content and potential measurement biases in hedge fund benchmarks. Hedge fund indices built from databases of individual hedge funds inherit the measurement biases in the databases. In addition, broad-based indices mask the diversity of individual hedge fund return characteristics. Consequently, these indices provide incomplete information to investors seeking diversification from traditional asset classes through the use of hedge funds. They propose the use of funds of hedge funds when constructing hedge fund benchmark. The argument made is that returns of fund-of-hedge funds can deliver a cleaner estimate of the investment experience of hedge fund investors than the traditional approach. In terms of risk characteristics, indices of funds of hedge funds are more indicative of the demand side dynamics driven by hedge fund investors' preferences than are broad-based indices. Therefore, indices of funds of hedge funds can provide valuable information for assessing the hedge fund industry's performance.

11.4. Survivorship bias

Hedge funds and CTAs have a much higher attrition rate compared to mutual funds. Fung and Hsieh [44] report an annual attrition rate of 19% for CTAs. Brown, Goetzmann, and Ibbotson [29] report an annual attrition rate of 20% for CTAs and about 14% for offshore hedge funds. Higher attrition rate in hedge funds raises concerns regarding survivorship bias, which occurs if the database only contains information on "surviving" funds, i.e., funds that continue to operate and report information to the database vendor. In contrast, there are "defunct" funds, which include funds that have stopped reporting to the database vendor because of bankruptcies or liquidations, mergers, changes in fund names, or voluntarily stoppages of reporting. Unlike mutual funds that are legally required to disclose their performance, hedge funds report only voluntarily. Hence, a well-performing fund may chose to stop reporting to a database vendor as it may not want to wish to attract more money after reaching a target asset size. Exclusion of such well-performing defunct funds generates an offsetting downward bias compared to poorly performing funds that generate an upward bias in the computation of survivorship bias.[1] Different authors have documented different estimates of survivorship bias, the main reasons being the use of different databases over different sample periods. Fung and Hsieh [44] find a survivorship bias as high as 0.29% per month or 3.48% per year for CTAs during 1989–1995. Later in Fung and Hsieh [47], they update these results for 1989–1997 period and find the survivorship bias to be about 3.6% per year. Using US Offshore Funds Directory, Brown, Goetzmann, and Ibbotson [29] document survivorship bias of about 3% per year for offshore hedge funds over 1989–1995. Interestingly, Fung and Hsieh [47] find similar survivorship bias across all hedge funds in TASS database during 1994–1998. Liang [74] examines the survivorship bias in hedge fund returns by comparing two large databases, namely HFR and TASS. He documents an annual survivorship bias of 2.24% per year. Edwards and Caglayan [41] document a similar figure of 1.84% per year. Results of survivorship bias by investment styles indicate that the biases are different across styles. Liang [74] shows that poor performance is the main reason for a fund's disappearance. Furthermore, there are significant differences in fund returns, inception date, NAV, incentive and management fees and investment styles for the 465 common funds covered by both databases. Mismatching between reported returns and the percentage changes in NAVs can partially explain the differences in returns. Amin and Kat [11] using TASS database over the period 1994–2001 estimate the survivorship bias to be around 2% per annum. They document this bias can increase to 4–6% for small, young, and leveraged funds. Although the estimates of survivorship bias in hedge funds vary across different studies, they are generally higher than similar estimates for

---

[1] Termination bias is a subset of survivorship bias and occurs when funds cease to exist or funds voluntarily stop reporting.

mutual funds, 0.5% per year [62], 0.8% per year [27], and 1.4% per year [83].

Ackermann, McEnally, and Ravenscraft [1] argue that survivorship bias and self-selection bias offset each other in their sample using data from HFR and Managed Account Reports (MAR). Self-selection bias exists because well-performed funds have less incentive to report data to vendors to attract potential investors. Ackermann, McEnally, and Ravenscraft [1] indicate that the survivorship bias is small at an average magnitude of 0.013% per month or 0.16% per year. Amin and Kat [11] document that survivorship bias also introduces a downward bias in the standard deviation, an upward bias in the skewness, and a downward bias in the kurtosis.

11.5. Stale price bias

Hedge funds invest in relatively illiquid securities for which market prices may not be always readily available. In order to report returns at all dates, the last price of the security is often used. This is referred to as stale price bias.

Asness, Krail, and Liew [16] argue that the presence of stale prices due to illiquidity or managed pricing can artificially reduce estimates of volatility and correlation with traditional indices. Hence, they propose that there may be significant lagged relations between market returns and reported hedge fund returns, rendering simple monthly regression betas understated. Using standard procedure of estimating regression with lagged market returns, they find that hedge funds have significant market exposures. However, the study by Asness, Krail, and Liew [16] has been criticized by Kazemi and Schneeweis [68] who show that the use of a multi-factor model based on contemporaneous and lagged values of the S&P 500 returns does not indicate stale prices but simply reflect a historical anomaly. They conduct empirical tests for two time periods – January 1994 to March 2003 and January 1999 to March 2003 to show that when additional months of data are added (October 2002 to March 2003) to the original Asness, Krail, and Liew [16] paper for the second time period, the impact of stale prices or smoothing is either reduced, eliminated, or even reversed. They claim that the basis for the different results is simple. The S&P 500 index achieved an extra negative return in August 1998. In the following months, fixed income arbitrage or other credit sensitive hedge fund strategies also had negative returns in response to the LTCM collapse. In any regression using lagged values of S&P 500 index, the negative S&P 500 index return in August 1998 is correlated with hedge fund strategies which had negative returns in the three months after August 1998. As a result, for hedge funds with credit sensitivity, the lagged relationship with the S&P 500 index is significant while for non-credit sensitive strategies, the lagged relationship is not significant.

The returns to hedge funds and other alternative investments are often highly serially correlated. Getmansky, Lo, and Makarov [56] explore several sources of such serial correlation and show that the most likely explanation is illiquidity exposure and smoothed returns. They propose an econometric model of return smoothing and develop estimators for the smoothing profile as well as a smoothing-adjusted Sharpe ratio. For a sample of 908 hedge funds drawn from the TASS database, they show that their estimated smoothing coefficients vary considerably across hedge-fund style categories and may be a useful proxy for quantifying illiquidity exposure.

11.6. Instant history bias

Instant history bias (or backfill bias) is the consequence of hedge funds choosing to enter the database after good performance with earlier good returns being backfilled between the fund's inception date and the date of fund's entry into the database. This can lead to an upward bias in the reported returns. Fung and Hsieh [47] compute an instant history bias of 1.4% per year for the TASS database over the period 1994 to 1998. Edwards and Caglayan [41] document the magnitude of this bias to be around 1.2% per year, using MAR database over January 1990 to August 1998.

11.7. Self-selection bias

As hedge funds voluntarily report to the data vendors, Self-selection bias may arise if only funds with good performance chose to be included in a database. This can lead to an upward bias in the reported historical performance of hedge funds. However, this upward bias is limited, as funds with good performance may sometimes chose not to publish their performance as they may have reached their goal in terms of assets under management or their target size and thus, may not wish to attract more investors. Fung and Hsieh [47] conclude that this bias is negligible based on such reasoning.

11.8. Multi-period sampling bias

Multi-Period sampling bias is not an artifact of how the data is collected by different database vendors. Instead, this bias is a result of imposing a requirement of certain length of return history for funds to be included in the sample. Usually, academic research requires a minimum of 24-month or 36-month returns for a fund to be included in the sample. Fung and Hsieh [47] conclude that this bias is small with its magnitude being close to 0.6% when a 36-month minimum return history is imposed. It should be noted that requiring longer return history also introduces survivorship bias as funds that did not survive for long periods get excluded from the sample.

References

[1] C. Ackermann, R. McEnally, and D. Ravenscraft, "The performance of hedge funds: Risk, return and incentives," *Journal of Finance*, vol. 54, no. 3, pp. 833–874, 1999.

[2] V. Agarwal and Narayan Y. Naik, "Multi-period performance persistence analysis of hedge funds," *Journal of Financial and Quantitative Analysis*, vol. 35, no. 3, pp. 327–342, 2000.

[3] V. Agarwal and Narayan Y. Naik, "Generalised style analysis of hedge funds," *Journal of Asset Management*, vol. 1, no. 1, pp. 93–109, 2000.

[4] V. Agarwal and Narayan Y. Naik, "On taking the alternative route: Risks, rewards and performance persistence of hedge funds," *Journal of Alternative Investments*, vol. 2, no. 4, pp. 6–23, 2000.

[5] V. Agarwal and Narayan Y. Naik, "Risks and portfolio decisions involving hedge funds," *Review of Financial Studies*, vol. 17, no. 1, pp. 63–98, 2004.

[6] V. Agarwal, Naveen D. Daniel, and Narayan Y. Naik, "Role of managerial incentives, flexibility, and ability: Evidence from performance and money flows in hedge funds," Working Paper, Georgia State University and London Business School, 2005.

[7] V. Agarwal, William H. Fung, Yee Cheng Loon, and Narayan Y. Naik, "Risks in hedge fund strategies: Case of convertible arbitrage," Working Paper, Georgia State University and London Business School, 2005.

[8] G. J. Alexander and A. M. Baptista, "Conditional expected loss as a measure of risk: Implications for portfolio selection," Working Paper, University of Arizona, 2002.

[9] G. S. Amin and H. M. Kat, "Portfolios of hedge funds: What investors really invest in," Working Paper, City University and University of Reading, 2002.

[10] G. S. Amin and H. M. Kat, "Stocks, bonds and hedge funds: Not a free lunch!," Working Paper, City University and University of Reading, 2002.

[11] G. Amin and H. Kat, "Welcome to the dark side: Hedge fund attrition and survivorship bias over the period 1994–2001," Working Paper, ISMA Centre, University of Reading, 2002.

[12] G. S. Amin and H. M. Kat, "Hedge fund performance 1990–2000: Do the money machines really add value?," *Journal of Financial and Quantitative Analysis*, vol. 38, no. 2, pp. 251–274, 2003.

[13] M. J. P. Anson, "Hedge fund incentive fees and the 'free option'," *Journal of Alternative Investments*, Fall, pp. 43–48, 2001.

[14] G. O. Aragon, "Timing multiple markets: Theory and evidence," Working Paper, Boston College, 2003.

[15] G. O. Aragon, "Share restrictions and asset pricing: Evidence from the hedge fund industry," Working Paper, Boston College, 2004.

[16] C. Asness, R. Krail, and J. Liew, "Do hedge funds hedge?," *Journal of Portfolio Management*, vol. 28, no. 1, pp. 6–19, 2001.

[17] W. Bailey, H. Li, and X. Zhang, "Hedge fund performance evaluation: A stochastic discount factor approach," Working Paper, Cornell University, 2004.

[18] T. G. Bali, S. Gokcan, and B. Liang, "Value at risk and the cross section of hedge fund returns," Working Paper, Baruch College and University of Massachusetts, Amherst, 2005.

[19] P.-A. Barès, R. Gibson, and S. Gyger, "Performance in the hedge funds industry: An analysis of short- and long-term persistence," *Journal of Alternative Investments*, Winter, pp. 25–41, 2003.

[20] P.-A. Barès, R. Gibson, and S. Gyger, "Style consistency and survival probability in the hedge funds' industry," Working Paper, Swiss Banking Institute, 2001.

[21] G. Baquero, J. ter Horst, and M. Verbeek, "Survival, look-ahead bias, and the persistence in hedge fund performance," *Journal of Financial and Quantitative Analysis*, vol. 40, no. 3, pp. 493–517, 2005.

[22] Z. Bodie, A. Kane, and A. J. Marcus, *Investments*, McGraw-Hill Companies Inc., 2002.

[23] O. Bondarenko, "Market price of variance risk and performance of hedge funds," Working Paper, University of Illinois, Chicago, 2004.

[24] N. M. Boyson, "Another look at career concerns: A study of hedge fund managers," Working Paper, Northeastern University, 2005.

[25] N. M. Boyson and M. J. Cooper, "Do hedge funds exhibit performance persistence? A new approach," Working Paper, Northeastern University and Purdue University, 2004.

[26] C. Brooks and H. M. Kat, "The statistical properties of hedge fund index returns and their implications for investors," Working Paper, City University, 2001.

[27] S. J. Brown and W. N. Goetzmann, "Performance persistence," *Journal of Finance*, vol. 50, pp. 679–698, 1995.

[28] S. J. Brown and W. N. Goetzmann, "Hedge funds with style," *Journal of Portfolio Management*, vol. 29, no. 2, pp. 101–112, 2003.

[29] S. J. Brown, W. N. Goetzmann, and R. G. Ibbotson, "Offshore hedge funds: Survival and performance 1989–1995," *Journal of Business*, vol. 72, no. 1, pp. 91–117, 1999.

[30] S. J. Brown, W. N. Goetzmann, and B. Liang, "Fees on fees in funds of funds," *Journal of Investment Management*, vol. 2, no. 4, pp. 39–46, 2004.

[31] S. J. Brown, W. N. Goetzmann, and J. Park J., "Careers and survival: Competition and risk in the hedge fund and CTA industry," *Journal of Finance*, vol. 56, no. 5, pp. 1869–1886, 2001.

[32] M. K. Brunnermeier and S. Nagel, "Hedge funds and the technology bubble," *Journal of Finance*, vol. 59, no. 5, pp. 2013–2040, 2004.

[33] M. Carhart, "On persistence in mutual fund performance," *Journal of Finance*, vol. 52, no. 1, pp. 57–82, 1997.

[34] N. Chan, M. Getmansky, S. M. Haas, and A. W. Lo, "Systemic risk and hedge funds," Working Paper, MIT and University of Massachusetts, Amherst, 2005.

[35] Y. Chen, "Timing ability in the focus market of hedge funds," Working Paper, Boston College, 2004.

[36] J. Cvitanic, A. Lazrak, L. Martellini, and F. Zapatero, "Optimal investment in alternative portfolio strategies," Working Paper, University of Southern California, 2001.

[37] R. J. Davies, H. M. Kat, and S. Lu, "Fund of hedge funds portfolio selection: A multiple-objective approach," Working Paper, City University, 2004.

[38] R. J. Davies, H. M. Kat, and S. Lu, "Single strategy funds of hedge funds," Working Paper, City University, 2004.

[39] A. B. Dor and R. Jagannathan, "Understanding mutual fund and hedge fund styles using return based style analysis," Working Paper, Northwestern University, 2002.

[40] A. B. Dor, R. Jagannathan, and Iwan Meier, "Understanding mutual funds and hedge funds styles using return-based style analysis," *Journal of Investment Management*, vol. 1, no. 1, pp. 97–137, 2003.

[41] F. R. Edwards and M. O. Caglayan, "Hedge fund performance and manager skill," *Journal of Futures Markets*, vol. 21, no. 11, pp. 1003–1028, 2001.

[42] B. Eichengreen and D. Mathieson, "Hedge funds and financial market dynamics," Occasional Paper 166, International Monetary Fund, 1998.

[43] W. Fung and D. A. Hsieh, "Empirical characteristics of dynamic trading strategies: The case of hedge funds," *Review of Financial Studies*, vol. 10, no. 2, pp. 275–302, 1997.

[44] W. Fung and D. A. Hsieh, "Survivorship bias and investment style in the returns of CTAs," *Journal of Portfolio Management*, vol. 24, no. 1, pp. 30–41, 1997.

[45] W. Fung and D. A. Hsieh, "Is mean-variance analysis applicable to hedge funds?," *Economic Letters*, vol. 62, no. 1, pp. 53–58, 1999.

[46] W. Fung and D. A. Hsieh, "Measuring the market impact of hedge funds," *Journal of Empirical Finance*, vol. 7, no. 1, pp. 1–36, 2000.

[47] W. Fung and D. A. Hsieh, "Performance characteristics of hedge funds and CTA funds: Natural versus spurious biases," *Journal of Financial and Quantitative Analysis*, vol. 35, no. 3, pp. 291–307, 2000.

[48] W. Fung and D. A. Hsieh, "The risk in hedge fund strategies: Theory and evidence from trend followers," *Review of Financial Studies*, vol. 14, no. 2, pp. 313–341, 2001.

[49] W. Fung and D. A. Hsieh, "Asset-based factors for hedge funds," *Financial Analysts Journal*, vol. 58, no. 5, pp. 16–27, 2002.

[50] W. Fung and D. A. Hsieh, "Hedge-fund benchmarks: Information content and biases," *Financial Analysts Journal*, vol. 58, no. 1, pp. 22–34, 2002.

[51] W. Fung and D. A. Hsieh, "Risk in fixed-income hedge fund styles," *Journal of Fixed Income*, vol. 12, no. 2, pp. 1–21, 2000.

[52] W. Fung and D. A. Hsieh, "Extracting portable alphas from equity long/short hedge funds," *Journal of Investment Management*, vol. 2, no. 4, pp. 1–19, 2004.

[53] W. Fung and D. A. Hsieh, "Hedge fund benchmarks: A risk based approach," *Financial Analysts Journal*, vol. 60, no. 5, pp. 65–80, 2004.

[54] W. Fung, D. Hsieh, N. Naik, and T. Ramadorai, "Lessons from a decade of hedge fund performance: Is the party over or the beginning of a new paradigm?," Working Paper, Duke University and London Business School, 2005.

[55] H.-G. Fung, X. E. Xu, and J. Yau, "Global hedge funds: Risk, return, and market timing," *Financial Analysts Journal*, pp. 19–30, Nov/Dec, 2002.

[56] M. Getmansky, "The life cycle of hedge funds: Fund flows, size and performance," Working Paper, University of Massachusetts, Amherst, 2004.

[57] M. Getmansky, A. W. Lo, and I. Makarov, "An econometric model of serial correlation and illiquidity in hedge fund returns," *Journal of Financial Economics*, vol. 74, no. 3, pp. 529–609, 2004.

[58] M. Getmansky, A. W. Lo, and S. X. Mei, "Sifting through the wreckage: Lessons from recent hedge-fund liquidations," Working Paper, MIT and University of Massachusetts, Amherst, 2004.

[59] D. Giamouridis and I. D. Vrontos, "Hedge funds portfolio construction: A dynamic approach," Working Paper, Athens University of Economics and Business and City University, 2005.

[60] W. N. Goetzmann, J. E. Ingersoll, and S. A. Ross, "High-water marks and hedge fund management contracts," *Journal of Finance*, vol. 58, no. 4, pp. 1685–1717, 2003.

[61] W. N. Goetzmann, J. E. Ingersoll, M. Spiegel, and I. Welch, "Sharpening sharpe ratios," Working Paper, Yale University, 2002.

[62] Mark Grinblatt and Sheridan Titman, "Mutual fund performance: An analysis of quarterly portfolio holdings," *Journal of Business*, vol. 62, pp. 393–416, 1989.

[63] A. Gupta and B. Liang, "Do hedge funds have enough capital? A value-at-risk approach," *Journal of Financial Economics*, vol. 77, pp. 219–253, 2005.

[64] N. Hagelin and B. Pramborg, "Evaluating gains from diversifying into hedge funds using dynamic investment strategies," Working Paper, Stockholm University, 2003.

[65] M. J. Howell, "Fund age and performance," *Journal of Alternative Investments*, vol. 4, no. 2, Fall, pp. 57–60, 2001.

[66] P. Jorion, "Risk management lessons from Long-Term Capital Management," *European Financial Management*, vol. 6, no. 3, pp. 277–300, 2000.

[67] H. M. Kat and F. Menexe, "Persistence in hedge fund performance: The true value of a track record," Working Paper, City University, 2002.

[68] H. Kazemi and T. Schneeweis, "Hedge funds: Stale prices revisited," Working Paper, University of Massachusetts, Amherst, 2004.

[69] F. Koh, W. T. H. Koh, and M. Teo, "Asian hedge funds: Return persistence style and fund characteristics," Working Paper, Singapore Management University, 2003.

[70] R. Kosowski, N. Y. Naik, and M. Teo, "Is stellar hedge fund performance for real?," Working Paper, INSEAD, London Business School, and Singapore Management University, 2004.

[71] R. Kouwenberg and W. T. Ziemba, "Incentives and risk taking in hedge funds," Working Paper, Erasmus University and University of British Columbia, 2004.

[72] F.-S. Lhabitant and M. Learned, "Hedge fund diversification: How much is enough?," Working Paper, Thunderbird School of Management, 2002.

[73] B. Liang, "On the performance of hedge funds," *Financial Analysts Journal*, vol. 55, no. 4, pp. 72–85, 1999.

[74] B. Liang, "Hedge funds: The living and the dead," *Journal of Financial and Quantitative Analysis*, vol. 35, no. 3, pp. 309–326, 2000.

[75] B. Liang, "The accuracy of hedge fund returns," *Journal of Portfolio Management*, vol. 29, no. 3, pp. 111–122, 2003.

[76] B. Liang, "Alternative investments: CTAs, hedge funds and fund-of-funds," Working Paper, University of Massachusetts, Amherst, 2003.

[77] J. Liew, "Hedge fund index investing examined," *Journal of Portfolio Management*, vol. 29, no. 2, pp. 113–123, 2003.

[78] A. W. Lo, "The statistics of Sharpe Ratios," *Financial Analysts Journal*, vol. 58, no. 4, pp. 36–52, 2002.

[79] A. W. Lo, "Risk management for hedge funds: Introduction and overview," *Financial Analysts Journal*, vol. 57, no. 6, pp. 16–33, 2001.

[80] A. Lucas and A. Siegmann, "Explaining hedge fund investment strategies by management reward structures," Working Paper, Vrije Universiteit, Amsterdam, 2002.

[81] A. Lucas and A. Siegmann, "Hedge fund payoffs and loss aversion," Working Paper, Vrije Universiteit, Amsterdam, 2003.

[82] B. Maillet and P. Rousset, "Classifying hedge funds: An application of kohonen map," Working Paper, University of Paris, Pantheon-Sorbonne, 2001.

[83] Burton Malkiel, "Returns from investing in equity mutual funds 1971 to 1991," *Journal of Finance*, vol. 50, pp. 549–572, 1995.

[84] R. C. Merton, "On market timing and investment performance I: An equilibrium theory of value for market forecasts," *Journal of Business*, vol. 54, pp. 363–406, 1981.

[85] M. Mitchell and T. Pulvino, "Characteristics of risk in risk arbitrage," *Journal of Finance*, vol. 56, no. 6, pp. 2135–2175, 2001.

[86] P. Monteiro, "Forecasting hedge funds volatility: A risk management approach," Working Paper, ISCTE, 2004.

[87] N. Naik, M. Stromqvist, and T. Ramadorai, "Learning while investing: Characterizing hedge fund investor behaviour," Working Paper, BNP Paribas Hedge Fund Centre, London Business School, 2005.

[88] S. Panageas and M. M. Westerfield, "High water marks: High risk appetites? Hedge fund compensation and portfolio choice," Working Paper, University of Southern California and Wharton School, 2004.

[89] A. J. Patton, "Are 'market neutral' hedge funds really market neutral?," Working Paper, London School of Economics, 2004.

[90] T. Schneeweis and R. Spurgin, "Multifactor analysis of hedge fund, managed futures, and mutual fund return and risk characteristics," *Journal of Alternative Investments*, pp. 1–24, 1998.

[91] W. F. Sharpe, "Asset allocation: Management style and performance measurement," *Journal of Portfolio Management*, vol. 18, pp. 7–19, 1992.

Editorial Scope

Foundations and Trends® in Finance will publish survey and tutorial articles in the following topics:

- Corporate Governance
- Corporate Financing
- Dividend Policy and Capital Structure
- Corporate Control
- Investment Policy
- Agency Theory and Information
- Market Microstructure
- Portfolio Theory
- Financial Intermediation
- Investment Banking
- Market Efficiency
- Security Issuance
- Anomalies and Behavioral Finance
- Asset-Pricing Theory
- Asset-Pricing Models
- Tax Effects
- Liquidity
- Equity Risk Premium
- Pricing Models and Volatility
- Fixed Income Securities
- Computational Finance
- Futures Markets and Hedging
- Financial Engineering
- Interest Rate Derivatives
- Credit Derivatives
- Financial Econometrics
- Estimating Volatilities and Correlations

Information for Librarians

Foundations and Trends® in Finance, 2005, Volume 1, 4 issues. ISSN paper version 1567-2395 (USD 300 N. America; EUR 300 Outside N. America). ISSN online version 1567-2409 (USD 300 N. America; EUR 300 Outside N. America). Also available as a combined paper and online subscription (USD 340 N. America; EUR 340 Outside N. America).

Foundations and Trends® in
Finance
Vol 1, No 2 (2005) 103-169

Hedge Funds

Vikas Agarwal[1] and Narayan Y. Naik[2]

[1] Georgia State University, Robinson College of Business, 35, Broad Street, Suite 1221, Atlanta GA 30303, USA, vagarwal@gsu.edu
[2] London Business School, Sussex Place, Regent's Park, London NW1 4SA, UK, nnaik@london.edu

Abstract

Hedge Funds summarizes the academic research on hedge funds and commodity trading advisors. The hedge fund industry has grown tremendously over the recent years. According to some industry estimates, hedge funds have increased from USD 39 million in 1990 to about USD 972 million in 2004 and the total number of hedge funds has gone up from 610 to 7,436 over the same period. At the same time, hedge fund strategies have changed significantly. In 1990 the macro strategy dominated the industry while in 2004 the equity hedge strategy had the largest share of the market. There has also been a shift in the type of investor in hedge funds. In the early 1990s the typical investor was a high net-worth individual investor, today the typical investor is an institutional investor. Thus, the hedge fund market has not only grown tremendously, but the nature of the market has changed.

Despite the enormous growth of this industry, there is limited information available on hedge funds. As a result, there is a need for rigorous research from both the investors' and regulators' point of view. Investors need research to better understand their investment and their risk exposure. This research also helps investors recognize the extent of diversification benefits hedge funds offer in combination with investments in traditional asset classes, such as stocks and bonds. Regulators can use this research to identify situations where regulation may be needed to protect investors' interests and to understand the impact hedge funds trading strategies have on the stability of the financial markets.

The first part of *Hedge Funds* summarizes hedge fund performance, including comparisons of risk-return characteristics of hedge funds with those of mutual funds, factors driving hedge fund returns, and persistence in hedge fund performance. The second part reviews research regarding the unique contractual features and characteristics of hedge funds and their influence on the risk-return tradeoffs. The third part reviews the role of hedge funds in a portfolio including the extent of diversification benefits and limitations of standard mean-variance framework for asset allocation. Finally, the authors summarize the research on the biases in hedge fund databases.

CPSIA information can be obtained at www.ICGtesting.com
Printed in the USA
BVOW012004231212

308908BV00002BA/17/A